Head Strong

How to Get Physically and Mentally Fit

Tony Buzan

Thorsons

dedication

To **Sir Steven Redgrave, CBE**, five times Olympic Gold Medallist, Brain Trust Charity "Brain of the Year" 1997, in appreciation of his prodigious mental and physical accomplishments, and the supremely positive example he has given the world and the future in the application of Body Thinking and Mind Power.

Thorsons
An Imprint of HarperCollins*Publishers*
77–85 Fulham Palace Road
Hammersmith, London W6 8JB

The Thorsons website address is:
www.thorsons.com

and *Thorsons is a trademark of HarperCollins Publishers Limited*

First published 2001

10 9 8 7 6 5 4 3 2 1

©Tony Buzan 2001

Tony Buzan asserts the moral right to be
identified as the author of this work

Mind Maps® is a registered trade mark of the Buzan Organization

Mind Map® illustrations by Alan Burton
Text illustrations by Alan Burton, Peter Cox Associates, Jeff Edwards and Jennie Dooge

A catalogue record of this book is
available from the British Library

ISBN 0 00 711397 8

Printed and bound in Italy

contents

list of Mind Map® plates

appreciation

I would like to thank especially all those kind people who have helped me make *Head Strong* as strong as it has become...

Yildiray Acar, for the use of his beautiful Aegean island Tersane Adasi, where portions of this book were written; my dear friend Sean Adam, for constantly provoking me to make the most of my own mind and body; Joe Adams, who, as Managing Director of Encyclopaedia Britannica UK, provided the initial encouragement for the book that gave birth to this one; Mohammed Abdullah Moubarak Al Sabah, for his enlightening insights on the synergetic principle and for his encouragement; my Medhufushi friends Ray Butler, Brian Logan and Aki, who so magnificently supported me on the final run in; my 97-year-old friend and neighbor, Tom Benning, my mentor, guide and exemplar in matters of the mind and body; my Personal Assistant and friend Lesley Bias, who created the manuscript for this book and whose decade-long support has enabled me to make the most of my own mind and body; Alan Burton, for his witty, creative and masterful illustrations and Mind Maps®; John Bush, Salatticum Poet, for his on-going friendship and help in the development of my poetic and martial artist souls; Professor Barry Buzan, my beloved and dedicated brother, who has so regularly and patiently helped me to make both small and great leaps in the development and beneficial utilization of my own intelligence; my dear mother Jean Buzan, who carefully nurtured my own developing mind, and who has painstakingly and ferociously edited this book at every stage of its genesis; the Buzan Centres Worldwide and all the BLIs (Buzan Licensed Instructors), for their on-going commitment to the development of a Mentally Literate Planet; Jeremy Cartland, Salatticum Poet, for his metaphoric inspiration; Craig Collins, who helped me open up Asia, Australia and New Zealand to the ideas contained in this book; Paul Collins (dec.), my dear departed athletic, Alexander, poise, physical and psychological coach; the Folley family for providing me, for 20 years, the paradisial environment which has been so instrumental in allowing me to incubate many of the ideas which appear in this book; Michael J. Gelb, Brain of the Year 1999, for being a living example to millions of people around the world of making the most of your mind and body; Lorraine Gill the artist, for her unstinting help in opening my "Doors of Perception"; Mustafa and Dojan Guneri, for their support and for the use of their beautiful sailing barque, Kaya Guneri II, which was the "traveling home" for much of the conception and completion of Head Strong; Helga Hampton, for preparing the first embryonic manuscript, and for her on-going faithfulness to Mental Literacy; "Superman" Robert Heller, for his on-going support of the ideal; Ted Hughes (dec.), Poet Laureate, for being my constant poetic and personal inspiration and for his life-long dedication to producing "Warriors of the Mind"; Grandmaster Raymond Keene OBE, for his friendship and his on-going super-stimulation of my own thinking processes, and for his mentoring in the Mental Martial Arts of Mind Sports; my External Editor-in-Chief and companion Vanda North, Head of Buzan Centres Worldwide, for her inspiration of and dedication to this new book, including the original Mind Map transcription; Robert Ornstein for his personal encouragement, and for his inspirationally illustrated, written and amazing works on our Amazing Brains; Robyn Pontynen and all the staff at Lizzard Island, for supplying me with the physical, mental and personal support during the writing of the manuscript, and for providing me the "studio" in which much of it was written; Sir Brian and Lady Mary Tovey, for their unswerving trust in my own brain, and the brains of everyone on Planet Earth; and Nicholas Wade, for his on-going instructions in the delights of literary inventiveness.

•   •   •

I would also like to thank my Publications Manager, Caroline Shott, and my editorial and publishing team at Thorsons, who once again have been masterful in helping this dream come to fruition: my Commissioning Editor, Carole Tonkinson; my Editor, Charlotte Ridings; Stephen Bray; Paul Redhead; Toby Watson; Tim Byrne; Yvette Cowles; Jo Lal; Megan Slyfield; Jacqui Caulton; Aislinn McCormick; and Ariel Kahn.

preface sir steven redgrave, CBE

When I first started my career I thought all I had to do was get out there training, practice my rowing and build up my muscle strength.

It soon became increasingly clear to me that there was much more:

- how important it was to understand the different ways in which my body *responded* to the training
- how I could develop key muscle areas important for my sport, and
- how my diet had a major part to play.

But more than anything else, I came to realize the effect my brain had upon my body. How my brain influenced my body development and how winning was all about what was happening in my mind. From that point, it became a *total* training program for me, of both my body and my mind.

Tony Buzan is one of the very few people I have met who really understands so completely how important the brain is to any sportsman or woman. As I said to Tony when he asked me about what's going on in an Olympic rowing final, "Tony, it's mainly a 'Battle of the Brains.'"

This book is going to be a breakthrough for anyone who wants to go out there and win and for anyone wanting a fitter, healthier and more successful life.

The (next) great phase in man's development (is) when he passes from subconscious, to conscious control of his mind and body.

Matthias Alexander

a letter to my readers

When I was young I was continually questioning authority, asking "Who says who is intelligent or not?" and "What is intelligence, and can it be trained and improved?" I was also singularly un-athletic, and hated all forms of physical sports, which were obligatory at school!

At the age of 13 my life and attitudes were transformed. I had vaguely begun to realize that a fit body was attractive to girls! An athletic friend of mine introduced me to push-ups, chin-ups and sit-ups. In the cooperative/competitive nature of friends, we began to compare notes, and I tried to match him.

At first my performances were pathetic!

Gradually though, as I persisted, my results improved. Then came the "WOW!" When checking in the mirror I could see, for the first time in my life, the faint outline of my abdominal muscles (the "six-pack") and the first definition of the muscles in my chest, shoulders and arms.

I was transforming!

And I was transformed...

I began to realize that the body with which I had been blessed was not simply "there" – it was a flexible "machine" which would respond to the way I treated it. It was mine to abuse, lose, or use.

Suddenly a whole new world opened up to me, and I embraced it with gusto. Physical training was not the pain, agony and torture that I had imagined it to be in my earlier years. It was energizing, stress-reducing, and had made me both look and feel good.

I qualified as a lifeguard, studied the martial arts of ju-jitsu, karate, and eventually the "King of the Martial Arts" – aikido, and became an enthusiastic runner and rower. In conjunction with this I became a trainer in a health club, and kept myself further in shape by taking up disco and ballroom dancing (among the hardest physical sports there are!)

This eventually led me to assist in the coaching of Olympic athletes.

As I began to notice the first changes in my body as a young teenager, I began to ask the next question: "If I can transform my *body's* strength and power, then why cannot I transform my *brain's* strength and power too?"

The answer, of course, is that I could!

Not only that – the two were linked.

If you exercise your brain you will positively influence your body

If you exercise your body you will positively influence your brain

In harmony with my own physical development and self-exploration, including my many learning mistakes, I realized that those thinking tools that I had yearned for *did* exist; that I could convert stress and anger into energy and excitement; that there *were* thinking tools which could help guarantee me greater success; that there were techniques for improving all levels of physical and mental performance; and there was *always* a "brighter side."

The power to change your body lies in knowing how to use the power of your mind.

No more broken New Year resolutions – here are the formulas for life!

My wish is that this book will make your journey a little easier than mine was, and that you will derive as much pleasure, benefit, and ecstasy from your discoveries as I did, and continue to do!

Tony Buzan

introduction

you and your body and mind

At the end of the 20th century the human race made
an astounding discovery: that the brain is actually
connected to the body! For the past two centuries
intellectual and physical activities have been
separated by a giant conceptual divide. *Head Strong*
puts the Humpty Dumpty pieces back together again,
and shows you the power of actively enhancing the
body/brain connection.

did you know?

- People have "miraculously" recovered from critical illnesses such as cancer, and have overcome severe disabilities, simply through sheer willpower – their brain's control over their body.

- You can affect "automatic" bodily processes like your temperature and heart beat, physical health and athletic performance solely through the power of your thoughts. In 1970, an Indian yogi, Swami Rama, caused two areas a couple of inches apart on his right hand to change temperature, in *opposite* directions. The rate of the temperature change was about 2°C (4°F) per minute, and he was able to maintain the change until there was a temperature difference of 5°C (10°F).

- The tennis player Billie Jean King was considered by her opponents to be almost unbeatable once she had mentally "programmed" her body to win, despite the fact that there was no particular physical area in which she was superior to everyone else.

In *Head Strong* I will acquaint you with the awesome power and potential of your body and mind.

Head Strong is devoted to **Body Thinking**. It focuses on developing the mental thinking skills that will help you keep your body (and mind!) in good health, and some health, training and conditioning advice designed to maximize your Physical and Mental Intelligence.

Head Strong tackles six main themes:

1. To introduce you to "the body" of your brain, its astounding power, and the magical capabilities of your brain cells.
2. To introduce you to five new Brain Principles:
   - **The Brain Principle of Synergy**
   - **The Brain Principle of Knowledge**
   - **The Brain Principle of Truth**
   - **The Brain Principle of Success**
   - **The Brain Principle of Persistence**

   These will help you to understand more how your brain works, and to make using it a lot easier.
3. To introduce you to two major new thinking skills: **Meta-Positive Thinking** and **Radiant Thinking**. Each of these will transform the way you think. **Meta-Positive Thinking** will give you infallible tools for achieving your goals, and **Radiant Thinking** will demonstrate to you that your Creative powers are potentially infinite.
4. To introduce you to the revolutionary **Learning and Physical Training Success Formula** – known as **TEFCAS** – specifically designed to help you both create success from failure and to build on all successes.
5. To help you nurture and develop your physical power, health and well-being by giving you state-of-the-art information on how to maintain your overall physical robustness and health, in the areas of: Poise; Aerobic fitness; Flexibility; Strength; Diet; Stress reduction and relaxation; Drugs; Sleep and rest; Sex; and Mental attitude.

6. To help you apply everything you will learn from *Head Strong* to give you a much more positive and comprehensive new perspective on yourself and everybody else.

I will introduce you to the study of **holanthropy**, a word that comes from the Greek *holos*, meaning "whole," and *anthropos*, meaning "human." In other words, **holanthropy** is the study of the whole human being – the study of the *brain* and its interrelated functions; the study of the *body* and its interrelated functions; and the study of the interrelated functions of *brain and body*.

This introduction is an overview of the entire contents of *Head Strong*, providing a chapter-by-chapter outline and summary of each important area covered. This section also covers some of the major features of *Head Strong*, each of which is designed to make your reading more easy, more entertaining, more enjoyable, and more applicable to your daily life.

your body's potential/your brain's potential

Your body is a miraculous organ of phenomenal complexity and staggering ability. You are made of multiple *trillions* of molecules, all inter-linked in complex different architectures. These networks combine to make a body so intricate that even our most advanced sciences cannot describe it nearly to the full.

In addition, every year, our physical boundaries are being pushed back. Without exception new world records are established on an annual basis in virtually every sport, and medicine is constantly uncovering staggering new examples of our body's physical subtleties and capabilities. Yet even now, the "strongest, fastest and highest" are estimated to be using only a fraction of their latent aptitudes!

Your brain is a sleeping giant. During recent years accelerating research in psychology, education, biology, neuro-physiology, and physics has shown that the potential of your brain is almost infinitely greater than was imagined just a few years ago. Even the commonly heard statement that we use on average only 1 percent of our brains is wrong – the truth is that we use even less! This may sound discouraging, but on reflection you will realize that it is extremely *en*couraging – it means that you have more than 99 percent of your potential still to use.

As Shakespeare said:

What a piece of work is man! How noble in reason! how infinite in faculty! in form, in moving, how express and admirable! in action how like an angel! in apprehension how like a god! the beauty of the world! the paragon of animals!

Hamlet, Act II, scene 2

Head Strong is designed to help you develop the astounding and untapped potential of your body and your brain, and more importantly, the inter-relationship between the two.

parts and chapters

Head Strong is divided into three main parts, and into nine chapters. I recommend that you first browse through the book, getting an overall feel for the content and layout, and marking any areas which are of special interest to you.When you have completed this browse, establish the goals you would like to accomplish by the end of your reading, and plunge in!

part i – your amazing brain

Part I is devoted to an extensive exploration of the state-of-the-art information on your brain, and how you can make the best and most profitable use of that information.

chapter 1 – your amazing synergetic brain and body

This chapter introduces you to the first of the Brain Principles that you will discover in *Head Strong* – **Synergy**. When you understand this principle, you will find that *all* learning tasks will be easier to understand and accomplish.

The **Synergy Principle** will help you understand and benefit from all the remaining chapters in *Head Strong*. It relates to everything that follows, both in this book and in your life!

chapter 2 – the body of your brain: downstairs, upstairs; hind and fore; left and right

In Chapter 2, I trace the historical evolution of your brain and look at the major steps in this development. I examine the different parts of your brain from bottom to top, describing each one and its functions, and show how you can use this knowledge to your best advantage. As well as 'bottom-to-top', we consider your hind and fore brains and their functions and use, and then cover, in considerable detail, what is commonly called our 'left and right' brains (more accurately, your incredibly complex, sophisticated, and powerful cerebral hemispheres): the latest stage in nature's development of biological intelligence.

chapter 3 – your super bio-computer chip: the brain cell

In Chapter 3 I introduce you to the second Brain Principle – the **Principle of Knowledge** – and answer the following questions:

- What actually is the human brain cell?
- How powerful is it?
- How many do I have?
- How do they interact?
- Are the brain cells of human beings and animals the same or different?
- How much can the brain take in and how many thoughts can it possibly have - can your brain get "full up?" Is there a limit to what you can know?
- Are my thoughts real? Can I control my thoughts?

I hope that you will be pleased, provoked, and probably awed by many of the answers.

part ii – brain and body thinking skills

Part II is devoted to an explanation of the fundamental nature of your thinking processes, especially the whole nature of **Creative and Radiant Thinking**. In this section I will show you how to improve and enhance these aspects of your intelligence.

chapter 4 – meta-positive thinking

In Chapter 4, I introduce you to a revolutionary approach to **Positive Thinking**. Through a series of games, I will help you to see which thinking techniques help you to learn and succeed, and which significantly increase your probability of failure! In this chapter you will come to see how the way in which you think can affect the physical structure of your brain. In very real terms, it can be not only a matter of failure or success, but a matter of life and death. Obviously, we choose success and life. The **Brain Principle of Truth** and its importance to **Meta-Positive Thinking** is also explored.

chapter 5 – creative & radiant thinking: using your mind to better your body

In this chapter I explore with you new ways of developing your **Creative Thinking** powers. The chapter starts with a Creativity Game that allows you to benchmark yourself – to establish your current levels of **Creative Thinking**, and to compare them with global averages. Through a series of creativity games I then challenge you to break the normal boundaries of creativity, and to become an Olympian Creative Thinker!

I will then introduce you to my Creative Mind Map®, the thinking tool that has been described as the "Swiss army knife for the brain and for thinking creatively." The Mind Map® is then used to show how you can progressively increase your knowledge by using this thinking tool, eventually allowing you to reach the "Holy Grail" for thinkers: the **Radiant Thinking Paradigm Shift**.

The chapter concludes with an introduction to that most powerful of thinking skills – the use of metaphor.

part iii – healthy body healthy mind: your physical health and well-being

In Part III, I will introduce you to the amazing **Success Formula – TEFCAS**. **TEFCAS** will help you to understand and improve your physical and your mental learning processes, and your well-being. I also introduce you to state-of-the-art information on the nurturing, maintenance and development of your physical health and well-being.

chapter 6 – the revolutionary success formula – TEFCAS

When you were at school, college or university, were you ever taught the nature of learning – the actual processes by which the brain acquires knowledge?

Were you taught what to expect of your learning curve of success, plotting it against time and the number of times you practiced and tried?

Were you taught about the nature of failure?

Were you taught how to *deal* with failure?

Were you taught about the nature of success?

Were you ever taught about the most important "formula of formulas" – the **Correct Learning Formula**?

In Chapter 6, I answer all these questions, directing you toward a life where your learning will be, increasingly, a success. I also introduce you to the vitally important **Brain Principles of Success** and **Persistence**.

chapter 7 – your body: how to develop and use it well

In this chapter I give you a complete guide to your body, *and* to the vexed question of what *is* the relationship between your body and your mind. I show how you can develop and use your body well, especially with regard to:

- Poise
- Aerobic Fitness
- Flexibility
- Strength

By the end of this chapter you will have learned the true definition of fitness, and will know how to stay in peak physical (and mental) condition.

chapter 8 – brain and body food

Chapter 8 looks at the important area of nutrition, and gives some guidelines toward a diet that will guarantee to feed both your body and brain.

chapter 9 – stress-busting, healing, and more...

In Chapter 9 I take you through important and controversial seas that wash up such questions as:

- How do I deal with mounting stress and reach a state of relaxation?
- What effect do various drugs have on my body and brain?
- How important is sleep and rest?

And, most importantly:
- How does my *attitude* affect my health and fitness?

features

Head Strong is liberally sprinkled with special features to help you with your progress in understanding yourself:

stories

Head Strong contains a number of pertinent and amusing stories that will give you a clearer perspective on how your body and brain function.

studies

The text is backed-up by scientific reports and quotes, which create a solid foundation for the information and processes you will be considering and exploring.

body and brain stars

In *Head Strong* I will introduce you to the inspiring lives and thoughts of famous athletes and thinkers who have brilliantly worked on the relationship between their body and brain.

quotations

Head Strong is liberally sprinkled with quotations that summarize and crystallize the ideas that are important for you in the development of your own body and brain.

quick brain-checks and games

These include quizzes and games which will allow you to benchmark your current levels of awareness, knowledge and skills, and to improve all three! Answers are given at the end of chapters.

illustrations

Throughout *Head Strong* you will find illustrations, diagrams, graphs, tables, and sketches, all designed to supplement and enhance the text, and to make the whole process of reading *Head Strong* more valuable and enjoyable.

Mind Maps®

Throughout the following chapters you will find examples of the ultimate thinking tool – the Mind Map®. Mind Maps® literally give you "a map of your thinking territory" and can condense pages of information into one simple, inter-linked diagram, which makes learning, memory and creativity far easier. This is because, as you will discover, the Mind Map® reflects on the page the internal workings of your mind.

brain boosters

Brain Boosters are sayings/statements/affirmations that will allow you to use your new knowledge of your brain cell function and **Meta-Positive Thinking** to imprint **Meta-Positive** thoughts increasingly into your brain, and thus dramatically increase your possibility of **Success**.

quick brain-check 1 – body and brain problems

On a sheet of paper note down, in expansive detail, all the problems you have in using your brain and body. Make sure that you are honest with yourself, and that you leave nothing out. The more you bring your problems to light, the easier it will be for you to solve them as you progress through *Head Strong*!

the problems

No matter how many problems you wrote down, don't be over-concerned. Although your list (and the list that follows of other people's problems) might seem a little daunting, there is still hope! As you will be realizing, your brain and body are capable of performing more than adequately, even when we put them through the standard lack of care, lack of training, abuse and pressures of our normal lives that give rise to so many of these problems.

The common global responses to this Brain-Check (see opposite) indicate that our underlying problem is that we have not really been given enough information about how we, as human beings, work.

We can be compared to the unfortunate owner of a Supersonic Jet who, not knowing how the magnificently designed and constructed flying machine works, unwittingly puts water in the fuel tanks and sand in the moveable parts – and then blames it for not working!

Obviously the Supersonic Jet does work. Similarly your brain and body do work, magnificently. It is simply a matter of feeding and fuelling them appropriately.

Below is a summary of those problems volunteered by thousands of people who have come on my courses, and those at the Buzan Centres. The universality of these problems is emphasized by the fact that these answers are given by people from five different continents: from business people, university students, children, politicians, teachers, professors, and workers and people of all ages. No matter what walk of life people come from, the patterns of their problems are identical.

the most common global problems with body and brain

A 30 year survey involving over 20,000 people from five continents

alertness

anxiety and useless worry

aptitude – basic lack of!

association – ability to make connections,
    especially new ones

attitude – fitting the right attitude for
    the right situation

boredom

clarity of thinking

concentration

coordination – physical

coordination – mental

decisiveness

depression

diet

discipline

energy – lack of

fatigue – general

fear of failure

fitness

flexibility – mental

flexibility – physical

focus

frustration

goal-setting

growing old – declining mental and
    physical abilities

health – general

imagination – lack of

impatience

laziness

learning

memory – declining powers of!

mental blocks

motivation – lack of

negative thinking

nerves

note-taking – difficulties with

panic

poise/posture

pressure

problem-solving abilities

self-belief

self-confidence

self-discipline

sex

shyness

sleep – not enough/interrupted/lack of

speed of learning

sports

stamina – mental

stamina – physical

strength

stress – in abundance

visualization – difficulties with

willpower – weak!

quick brain-check 2 – transforming problems into goals

Now that you have identified your "problems," prepare for the first lesson from *Head Strong* – to think *positively*. Look at each one of the problems you have listed, and transform it into a positive goal. For example, if you noted a lack of creativity as a problem, decide that, as of today, with the help of *Head Strong*, you are going to improve your creative thinking skills. Similarly, if you have noted that your physical health and strength are problems, decide that, as of today, (and again with the help of *Head Strong*), you are going to begin a *smart* program for developing your physical health and well-being.

You may think: "Ah yes, I've tried this before, decided to do something good, and it never works. What's the point of doing it again now?" There *is* a point! All you have to do now is to *decide* to improve. You don't have to do *anything* else! As you read through *Head Strong*, you will be taught the all-important method of transforming your commitment into real action. You will also learn that the mere act of deciding to commit to something is your necessary and first step on your path to action, and that the decision itself has already increased the probability that you will be successful. The fact that you are reading *Head Strong* and have got this far is a pretty good guarantee that you are going to make it!

The rest of *Head Strong* is devoted to helping you *achieve* all your goals, and to launching you on a life-long journey that will transform your mental and physical skills, and your very life.

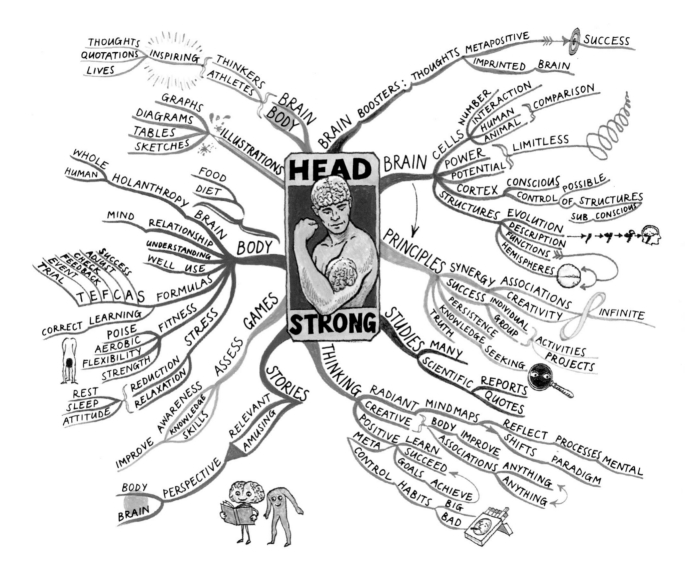

Mind Map® 1

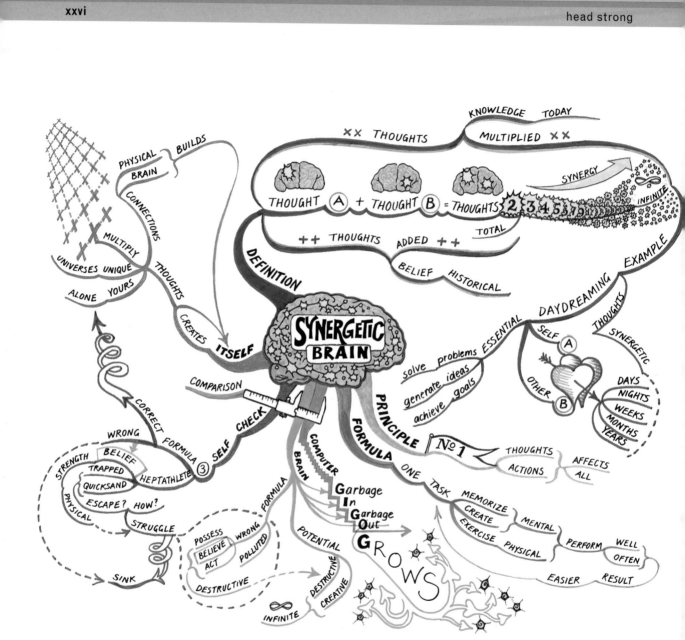

Mind Map® 2

your amazing brain

your amazing synergetic brain and body
the body of your brain
your super bio-computer chip

1

chapter one

your amazing synergetic brain and body

There is nothing either good or bad, but thinking makes it so.

(Hamlet, Act II, scene 2)

In this chapter I will introduce you to the first of the five **Brain Principles** in this book – **Synergy**. The **Synergy Principle** will reveal to you your infinite thinking ability, and your potential for lifelong improvement and success. I will guide you through the pitfalls of thinking, and show you, in passing, why sometimes especially the strong fail.

Knowledge of your brain, its processes and its use, is *mental literacy*. Mental Literacy®, as opposed to word literacy and numeracy (number literacy), refers to your ability to juggle the two "alphabets" of your brain. First is the alphabet of your *physical* brain: the lower and upper brains, the hind and fore brains, and the left and right brains (hemispheres) (this is explored in detail in Chapter 2). In addition, this alphabet includes your knowledge of the brain cell and its functions. Second is the alphabet of the *behaviors* of your brain, especially learning, thinking, the creative processes, memory, attitude (**meta-positive/negative thinking**), and the **Brain Principles**.

This knowledge about how your brain works can be likened to knowledge about how to drive a car. If you know how to drive you will be able to drive successfully. If you don't know how to drive, you will not get very far. The better your knowledge of driving and how to do it, the better at it you will be.

It is the same with your brain.

And even if you feel your brain is not a particularly good "model" don't be discouraged! It is commonly known that a Formula One racing driver in a battered old jalopy will still beat a relatively untrained driver in a Formula One car! The good news, as you will discover throughout *Head Strong*, is that you have a Formula One brain anyway. *Head Strong* is going to help you learn how to drive it like a champion!

It is essential to begin our journey with **Brain Principle Number 1, Synergy**, because this principle affects literally *everything* you do. If you don't know about this principle, you may become stuck in continual failure. On the other hand, knowledge of it will guide you to continual accomplishments and success.

brain principle number 1 – synergy

For thousands of years humans had thought that their thinking processes were organized on a simple, additive mathematical principle – every time you added a single new piece of data or new thought into the brain's computer, it simply added one more item to the store.

In the second half of the 20th century, however, we discovered that this was not the case, and in fact the brain operates *synergetically*. In a synergetic system the whole is greater than the sum of its parts; in other words 1 + 1 will equal *more* than 2. In such a system, "more" can reach Infinity.

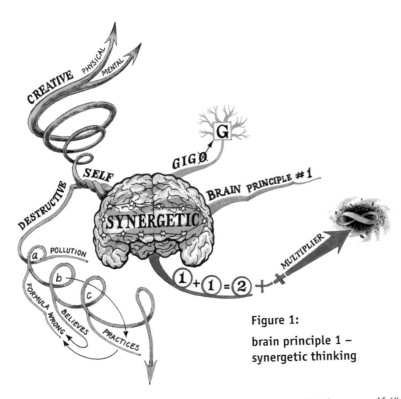

Figure 1:

brain principle 1 – synergetic thinking

Some of the first evidence for this came from Roger Sperry's work on the left and right brain, which won him a Nobel Prize, and which suggested that the brain was a *multiplying* mechanism rather than an adding machine. (See Chapter 2, page 21.)

How can this be so?

A simple example from everyday human activity will suffice: daydreaming! When you are daydreaming (which everyone does, every day!) you are engaging not in additive thinking behavior, but in multiplying, *synergetic* thinking.

For example, you will take yourself ("one") and someone else (another "one") and you will start to multiply your thoughts. Depending on the other "one" of your choice, you can daydream about yourself and that other "one" all day, all week, all month, all year, or, as some people do, all your lifetime! You can use the infinite theater of your imagination, and its infinite props, to create the most macabre and spine-chilling horror stories and tragedies, or the most glorious and uplifting comedies, romances, fairytales and epics. The productions of Hitchcock and Spielberg have *nothing* on your imagination.

From research such as Sperry's, from examples such as daydreaming, and from many other sources (a number of which you will discover in this book), we can confidently state that the potential for the human brain (*your* brain) to generate thought is, theoretically, *infinite*.

you are the architect of yourself

The consequence of this is both significant and profound; it will change the way you think – think about thinking, think about yourself, and think about others – *forever*. What it means is that your brain is *Self-Creating*. Every thought you think is unique to you, and fits into a network of other thoughts and associations that has never existed before and will never exist again, except in your own brain. Your thought then multiplies into the vast internet of your growing memories, fantasies, attitudes, and dreams. You are entirely and infinitely *unique*!

This news is made even more exciting by the realization that as you create more and more positive galaxies and universes of thought, you will at the same time be forging new physical connections within your brain. *You will literally be making your super bio-computer of a brain more complex, more sophisticated, more powerful, and more successful.*

In other words, the brain with which you read this now is not the same as it was yesterday, and will not be the same tomorrow.

You are the engineer and architect of your own physical brain, and the universes of thought that reside within it.

the learning secret

To make this growing good news even better, we can introduce an idea which will lay to rest many global misconceptions about your brain and body, and their aging and learning processes.

The more appropriately and well your brain does "X" then the easier "X" becomes

What does this mean? If, for example, "X" equals memory, then the more appropriately and well you practice using your memory, then the easier memorization will become. If "X" equals creativity, then the more appropriately you practice being creative, the more you will create and the more easy creative thinking will become. The more your body is used well, the more successful become its performances. The same principle obviously applies to learning, and to the development of all mental and physical skills.

The **Synergy Brain Principle** indicates that the pervading beliefs that creativity withers with age, and that other mental and physical skills necessarily decline, are dangerous misconceptions.

So far the news is all good. Let's next look at a little anagram slogan from the world of artificial intelligence: GIGO

GIGO is computer-speak for "Garbage In, Garbage Out!" You put garbage into your computer, you get garbage out of it...

For many years this was also thought to be true for the human brain. We (and you!) now know that this will not be the case. For in the case of the human brain it *must* be: GIG G.

Garbage In, Garbage Grows

How far can this garbage grow? *Infinitely*! Potentially infinite universes of garbage and rubbish are possible!

Armed with this new information we can reconsider the idea that our synergetic brain is self-creative and realize, more somberly, that, following the GIGG equation, the human brain can also be synergetically *destroyed* when rubbish or pollution infiltrates its incredibly sophisticated and complex systems.

And to what extent can this destruction expand? *Infinitely*! Just consider instances of suicides, murders, wars...

This is the bad news. However, there is some good news amidst the bad.

The fact that we know that our brains can be both infinitely creative and infinitely destructive, sheds some light on the centuries-old argument about the basic nature of humankind – whether or not humans are *fundamentally* aggressive, destructive and war-like, or rather more peaceful, cooperative and spiritual creatures.

If we were *fundamentally* aggressive and war-like, and as we are *infinitely* capable of destruction, we would no longer exist! We *do* exist, and therefore humankind must fundamentally veer toward a more enlightened nature.

There is more good news in the bad! The human brain is obviously not designed to self-destruct, otherwise *homo sapiens* would have terminated with the first couple!

Fortunately, the brain will only self-destruct in one circumstance, and that circumstance has three parts, which must all be present. The brain will self-destruct only *when it is polluted by the wrong formula*. It must, however, have more than just the wrong formula – it must *believe* in that wrong formula. In addition, the brain must *act* upon or *practice* that wrong formula.

The mind is its own place, and in it self,
Can make a Heav'n of Hell, a Hell of Heav'n.

Milton, *Paradise Lost*, Book I

quick brain-check 3 — correct formula

What do you think would happen in the following situation?

A particularly strong, flexible and fit heptathlete finds herself trapped in quicksand. Having always triumphed in physical situations by using her athletic and physical prowess, she is seduced into the *wrong formula* of thinking that the way to extricate herself from the situation is to struggle hard in order to get out.

Having regularly succeeded in the past she *believes* that this formula will help her succeed again. She therefore puts it into *practice*.

What will happen to her?

The answer is that she will *sink*. And *fast*!

The irony here is that the stronger and fitter she is, the *faster* she will sink. Why? Because she is putting *all* her massive resources and power, unwittingly, into exactly the *opposite* of what she wishes to achieve.

She is using the *wrong formula*.

•   •   •

As with our athlete, so it is with everything you think and do.

If your Brain and **Body Thinking** Formulas are Correct Formulas, then you will be whisked up into that positive-thinking and active spiral of the self-creative synergetic brain.

If you use Incorrect Formulas, then you will be caught in the negative vortex of synergetic self-destruction. (See Figure 1, page 5.)

I believe that in education, athletics, and the business and political worlds, we have been using formulas that, as with our heptathlete, *seemed* correct. Experience is increasingly showing that they are not. How we teach children to remember helps them progressively to forget; how we teach them to think encourages them to think less; how we react to their creativity increasingly negates that vital force; how we train their bodies leads them to ill health, injury or sloth; and our training of their attitudes leads them to ones which are unhealthy and negative rather than healthy and affirmative.

In *Head Strong* I will give you a safely guided tour through all your physical and mental worlds, showing you the correct formulas for positive- rather than negative-thinking, for creativity, for physical health and well-being on all levels, and for your ongoing success and growth in your body, mind, and spirit.

The adventure begins with some astounding revelations about the amazing body of your brain – the hardware for the software of your learning, thinking, creating, and physical self.

brain boosters

1. My brain is synergetic, allowing me to create infinite thoughts and associations.
2. I am in the process of creating *positively* synergetic thought-structures in my head.
3. My positive synergetic thoughts are getting stronger and stronger.
4. By good synergetic thinking I am actively changing and improving the physical structure and mental strength and power of my brain.

2

chapter two

the body of your brain: downstairs, upstairs; hind and fore; left and right

The brain regulates all bodily functions; it controls our most primitive behaviour – eating, sleeping, keeping warm; it is responsible for our most sophisticated activities – the creation of civilisation, of music, art, science and language. Our hopes, thoughts, emotions and personality are all lodged – somewhere – inside there. After thousands of scientists have studied it for centuries, the only word to describe it remains: 'AMAZING'.

Professor R. Ornstein, author of *The Psychology of Consciousness*

introduction

Recent surveys have showed that in most countries around the world, between 50 and 70 percent of people have some awareness of the fact that there is an "upper" and "lower" brain, and a "left" and "right" brain. However, the surveys also showed that only 10–20 percent actually knew any basic information about these two areas of which they were vaguely aware, and that less than 1 percent had actually done anything about improving their mental skills, behaviors, or life as a result of this new knowledge about their brains.

"Therein," as Shakespeare says, "lies the rub." To be aware of the existence of information is a fairly easy step. To know the actual content of that information is still quite easy. But to make the step from knowledge to affirmative action is the BIG step, and is the one that brings about change and positive development in your life and actions. It is this giant third step, leaping over the yawning chasm between knowledge and action, that this chapter in particular, and the rest of Head Strong, are devoted to helping you do.

In this chapter you will be introduced to the history of our knowledge of the brain, and then informed of state-of-the-art research about the "upper and lower brain" and the "left and right brain," which will dramatically improve your thinking skills. The chapter concludes with some amazing facts about your brain in comparison to the world's best computers, and some guidelines for improving your own performance on the basis of your new knowledge.

quick brain-check 4 — brain quotient!

Here is a quick quiz which will give you some idea about the state of your present knowledge on these vital areas of your brain and its functions. As you read through the chapter, the correct answers will become apparent. (If you want to check them immediately, the answers are on page 27!)

1. Your higher level thinking functions are controlled by the lower part of your brain. True/False?
2. The brain stem controls the brain's upper-level thinking systems. True/False?
3. In evolutionary terms, the front of the brain developed first. True/False?
4. The "cerebellum" is another word for the "cerebral cortex." True/False?
5. The lower brain is commonly referred to as the "Reptilian brain." True/False?
6. The limbic system maintains and adjusts posture and coordinates the muscular movement of the limbs. True/False?
7. The cerebral cortex is the part of the brain normally referred to as the "left/right brain." True/False?
8. The right cerebral cortex is the creative side of the brain. True/False?
9. The left cerebral cortex is the academic/intellectual side of the brain. True/False?
10. Your brain is hard-wired – there is not much you can do to change its abilities. True/False?
11. The world's best computers are now better than the human brain in their basic potentials. True/False?

our evolving knowledge of our evolving brains

Although the brain as we know it began evolving some 500 million years ago, the brain's knowledge of the brain has a much, much shorter history. As little as 2,500 years ago humankind knew virtually nothing about the brain and its internal workings. Before the Ancient Greeks, the mind was not even considered to be part of the human body, but was thought to exist as some form of ethereal vapor, gas or disembodied spirit.

Surprisingly, the Greeks did not get us that much further, and even Aristotle – their most famous philosophical thinker and the founder of modern science – concluded, after extensive investigations, that the center of sensation and memory was located in the heart!

Perhaps this idea is not that surprising, however. Imagine that you are a great Greek thinker, without the benefit of any of the knowledge of modern science or of any of its instruments (electron microscopes, brain scans, electroencephalograms, and the like) and that someone asks you to explain where the center of your senses, emotions and feelings, life force, and energy is located. Where would you logically assume it was? Quite "obviously" the center of your body, for it *is* the center, is the area that becomes physically active when you are emotional or exercise, has a constant "life beat," and is the place where, if a weapon pierces it, you are almost certain to die. With the head, however, often little appears to happen when a weapon pierces it. You do not necessarily die; you may simply become a little strange!

From the time of the Greeks to the beginning of the Renaissance in the late-14th century there was virtually no progress on brain-knowledge at all. During the Renaissance, a period of great intellectual awakening, it was finally realized that the center of thought and consciousness was located in the head, but the brain remained a mystery.

It was not until the 20th century that the really great strides forward in our understanding of our own brains were made, and many people still assume that it was in the first half of the century that the greatest advances were made. On the contrary; through the 1930s and 1940s we still believed the brain to be a simple machine, operating much like the very first computers, in which a few basic messages went in and were placed in the appropriate boxes, and that that was all there was to it. This model of the brain was common in basic psychology and educational textbooks until the late 1950s.

Only very recently were the really major breakthroughs in our knowledge and understanding made. These developments are so significant that they are already changing the foundations of psychology, education and business, and are emphasizing a fact sensed by many but until now impossible to "prove" – *the average brain is far more capable than we ever believed.*

A number of new findings stand out as particularly significant.

One of the most important developments is the awareness by the brain of the brain itself. Consider the following:

The universe, according to the latest research from the Hubble telescope, is approximately 13 billion years old; our own planet is 5 billion years old; life, amazingly, is 4.5 billion years old; the first basic brains appeared 500 million years ago; the appearance of the first *homo sapiens* was a mere 3 million years ago; the modern brain (the one with which you are reading this book!) evolved 50,000 years ago; civilization is, at most, on a global basis, 10,000 years old; the location of the human brain in the head was confirmed only 500 years ago; and **95 percent of all that the human race has ever discovered about the internal workings of its own brain has been discovered in the last 10 years!**

What this means is that the human race is at a turning-point in evolution, where we are suddenly discovering amazing facts about our own brains (your brain!) and are beginning to realize that the bio-computer we all have between our ears is infinitely more powerful than we had ever thought.

The Universe	13,000,000,000
Earth	5,000,000,000
Life	4,500,000,000
First Brains	500,000,000
Homo sapiens	3,000,000
Modern Brains	50,000
Civilization	10,000
Location of the Brain	500
95% of Knowledge of the Workings of the Brain	10
The Future	?
	??
	???

In addition to this astounding and revolutionary new interest in our own intelligence, there are three areas of *particular* interest: the "upper and lower brain," the "hind and fore brain," and the "left and right brain."

your lower and upper, hind and fore brains

You may have heard strange and mysterious stories about the inter-relationships between the lower and upper brain. In this section I will introduce you to what those parts really are, and how they relate together.

The brain evolved over 500 million years, and coincidentally developed simultaneously from bottom to top and from back to front (see Figure 2). Your brain evolved in the following order: first, the brain stem; second, the cerebellum, which was the hind brain; third, and slightly more forward in position, the limbic system, including the Thalamus and basal ganglia – the mid-brain; and finally, covering the rest of the brain and significantly forward in position, the universe's evolutionary masterpiece: your cerebrum or cerebral cortex.

Let's look at these parts in more detail, focusing on their place in evolutionary history, and their main functions. As you read, be amazed at how complicated and astonishing you actually are!

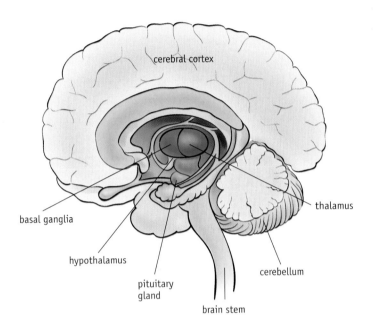

cerebral cortex

thalamus

basal ganglia

hypothalamus

cerebellum

pituitary gland

brain stem

**Figure 2:
the brain**

your brain stem

Evolved:	500 million years ago.
Common title:	Reptilian Brain or Primitive Brain.
Location:	Deep down in the brain, extending up from your spinal cord.
Functions:	Basic life support. Handles breathing and heart rate. Masterminds general level of alertness. Alerts you to important incoming sensory information. Controls

temperature. Controls the digestive process. Relays information from the cerebellum.

Interesting fact: Recent research seems to be suggesting that this area of your brain may be far more "intelligent" than we had previously thought.

Recent studies of the giant reptiles, such as alligators and crocodiles, whose entire brain is basically the brain stem, have shown that they have highly evolved forms of social behavior, deep family and group relationships, and emotions.

Next time you see one of these giant reptiles, live or on film, look more closely to see the magnificent brain stem in action!

the cerebellum

Evolved:	Approximately 400 million years ago.
Common title:	Little Brain or Hind Brain
Location:	Attached to the rear of the brain stem – part of the lower brain.
Function:	Controls body position, poise and balance. Monitors movement in space. Stores memories for basic learned responses. Transmits vital information via the brain stem to the brain.
Interesting fact:	In the human brain, the cerebellum has more than tripled in size in the last one million years.

the limbic system

Evolved:	Between 300 and 200 million years ago.
Common title:	Mammalian Brain or Mid Brain.
Location:	Between the brain stem and the cortex.
Function:	Maintains blood pressure, heart rate, body temperature, and blood sugar levels. Governs navigational skills in the hippocampus. Critical to learning and for short-term and

long-term memory and stores memories of life experiences. Maintains homeostasis (constant environment) in the body. Involved in survival emotions of sexual desire or self-protection.

Interesting facts:

1. Scientist Robert Ornstein says: "One way to remember limbic functions is that they are the four 'F's of survival: feeding, fighting, fleeing and sexual reproduction."

2. The limbic system contains the *hypothalamus*, often regarded as the most important part of the "mammalian brain." It is often known as the "brain" of the brain. Although tiny (about the size of half a sugar cube) and weighing only four grams, it regulates hormones, sexual desire, emotions, eating, drinking, body temperature, chemical balances, sleeping, and waking, while at the same time masterminding the master gland of the brain, the pituitary.

3. The *hippocampus* is increasingly thought to be the seat of learning and memory. In shape it looks remarkably like a little seahorse.

Two other major areas of the mid-brain include the *thalamus*, which makes preliminary classifications of external information reaching the brain, and which relays information to the cortex via the hypothalamus. It is the hypothalamus that is the part of your brain which decides what comes to your attention and what does not – for example, telling you at which moment to notice that the room is getting warmer or that you are getting hungrier!

The *basal ganglia*, which are located on both sides of the limbic system (as is the cerebellum), are concerned with movement control, especially initiating movements. In the human brain (your brain) these networks have been growing larger and more well developed over the last few million years.

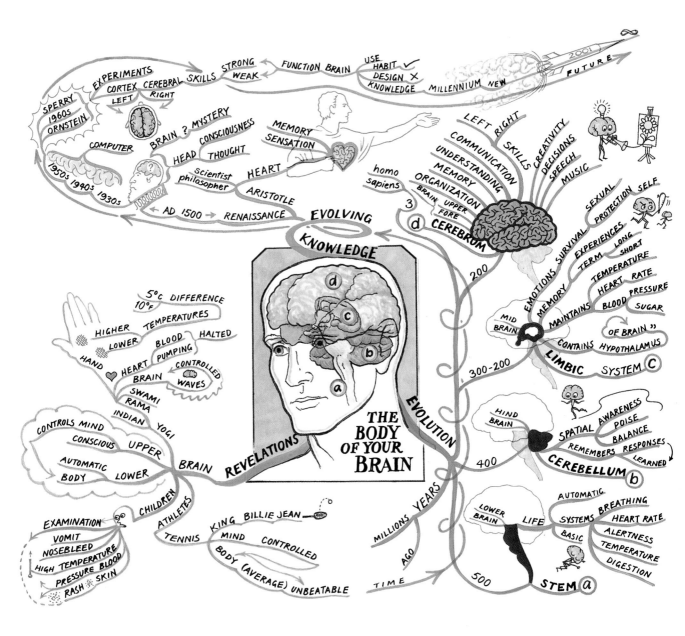

Mind Map® 3

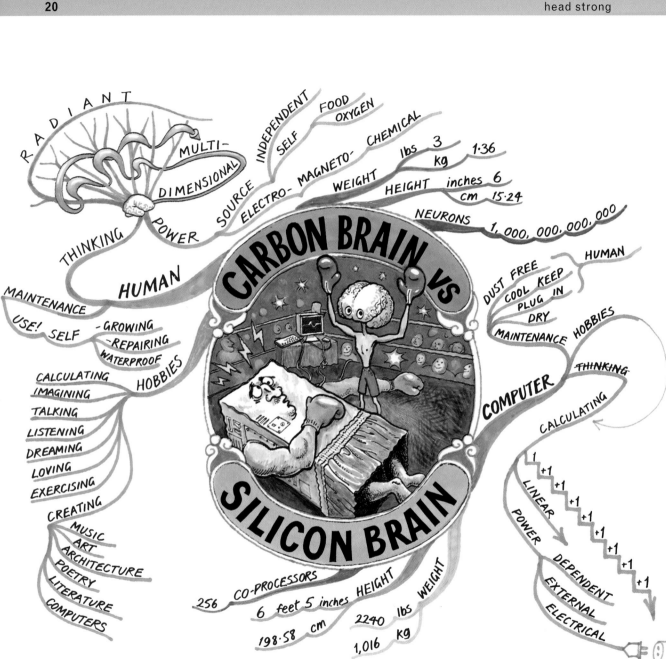

Mind Map® 4

the "left and right" brain
the cerebrum (cerebral cortex)

Evolved: Approximately 200 million years ago.

Common title: The left and right brain.

Location: Fits like a giant "thinking cap" over the entire brain; extends into the full area of your forehead.

Functions: Organization. Memory. Understanding. Communication. Creativity. Decision making. Speech. Music. Other specific functions include the full range of the "left/right brain" "cortical skills" discussed on page 22.

Interesting facts:

1. Your cerebrum is by far the largest part of your brain

2. The cerebrum is covered by that evolutionarily magical one-eighth inch thick, amazingly corrugated layer of nerve cells known as the cerebral cortex. It is the nature of our particular cortex that identifies you as human.

3. The two cerebral hemispheres are connected by a fabulously intricate network of nerve fibers called the *corpus callosum*; these 300 million nerve fibers shuttle information back and forward between the two hemispheres.

In the 1950s and 1960s Professor Roger Sperry, who received the Nobel Prize for his work, performed some incredible experiments on the cerebral cortex, in conjunction with Professor Robert Ornstein. They asked students to perform such varying mental tasks as daydreaming, calculating, reading, drawing, speaking, writing, coloring shapes, and listening to music, while measuring their brainwaves.

The results were a revelation. In general the cerebral cortex divides the tasks into two main categories – the left and the right (see Figure 3). The right tasks included rhythm, spatial awareness, Gestalt (whole picture), imagination, daydreaming, color, and dimension. The left included words, logic, numbers, sequence, linearity, analysis, and lists.

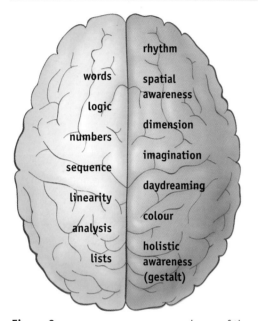

rhythm

words

spatial awareness

logic

dimension

numbers

imagination

sequence

daydreaming

linearity

colour

analysis

lists

holistic awareness (gestalt)

Figure 3:
right and left brain tasks

Ongoing research suggested that where people had been trained to use either "side" of their brain to the exclusion of the other, they tended to form Dominant Habits favoring those activities controlled by their chosen brain side, and to describe themselves in those terms.

The umbrella terms that evolved were "academic," "intellectual" and "business" for the left hemispheric activities, and "artistic," "creative" and "intuitive" for the right hemispheric activities. But these only gave part of the story.

Further research by Professor Ornstein and others revealed that the ongoing strength and weakness of the cortical skills in any one individual was more a function of habit than of basic brain design (see Chapter 4, page 53). When people who were weak in one area were trained in that area by experts, they invariably increased their skill and strength in that given area, and, what's more, *simultaneously strengthened their performance in other areas*! For example, if someone who had been weak in drawing skills was trained to draw and paint, their academic performance increased overall, especially in subjects such as geometry where perception and imagination are so important.

Another example is the right-brain skill of daydreaming, which is essential to your brain's survival. Daydreaming gives needed rest to those parts of your brain which have been doing more analytical and repetitious work, exercises your projective and imaginative thinking, and gives you a necessary chance to integrate and create. Most of the great geniuses used directed daydreaming to help them solve problems, generate ideas and achieve their great goals.

My own work in the fields of Creativity, Memory and Mind Mapping has led to identical conclusions. It has shown that by combining the elements of the two hemispheres, surprisingly huge increments in overall performance are achieved.

In the 20th century the world's educational systems unfortunately favored the "left brain" skills – mathematics, languages, and the sciences – over the arts, music, and the teaching of thinking skills, especially **Creative Thinking** skills. In focusing on only *half* of the brain's skills, it might appear that they were, literally, creating half-wits!

However, the truth of the matter is even worse. For as you now know from the **Brain Principle of Synergy** (see pages 4–8), the brain is a *multiplier*.

The left and right sides of your cerebral cortex shuttle messages back and forward between the hemispheres, creating a **Synergetic** formula for thinking and growth. By eliminating the possibility for this multiplying growth, it is not half-wits that are created, it is 1-percent-wits!

This makes the findings of the research into the great geniuses understandable. These studies have shown that, invariably, they used "both sides" of their brains. *Head Strong* encourages you also to use "both sides," "aft and fore" and "upstairs/downstairs," and thus to explore and develop your *own* genius.

downstairs/upstairs – some amazing revelations and stories

We have already seen, in the story of Indian yogi Swami Rama, how the upper brain can control the lower brain's "automatic" functions, such as the control of certain bodily processes.

In many "primitive" societies such abilities were taken for granted, although they were probably not related to the upper and lower brain. The Aborigines of Australia, for example, had what may be considered a far more advanced system of justice than that of some of our more recent Western societies. For instance, if a member of the tribe had committed an act which both the tribe and the individual thought was punishable by death, the tribe talked the matter over first and came to a unanimous agreement. If the convicted individual agreed with the tribe's conclusion, he then went to a flat area near the tribe's settlement, and sat down cross-legged. The tribe gathered in a large circle around him, and began to chant tribal songs. As they chanted, the convicted individual, using the power of his brain only, stopped all bodily processes one by one, until he had completed a self-induced execution.

Similar examples of the brain's extraordinary power are found in Western society. Very often, for example, when one partner in a very close relationship dies, the other, themselves often in good health, will say quite openly that they "want to go with him/her." Countless stories confirm that within a day or two the cortex has instructed all other brain systems to close down, and the surviving partner dies of what is commonly called a "broken heart," but which is increasingly known to be a love-directed brain.

the power of your brain versus the power of the computer

How powerful, then, is this super bio-computer you have in your head, in comparison to the new silicon brains?

Considering all you have learned about the computer and the brain, try the following Brain Game:

If the size of the world's most powerful computer in the year 2000 were represented by the size of a two-storey house, what size building would represent the potential power of your own brain:

(a) A miniature toy house?

(b) A doll's house?

(c) A house the size of a normal room?

(d) An apartment?

(e) A normal two-storey house?

(f) A mansion?

(g) A palace?

(h) A 100-storey skyscraper?

(i) Bigger than all the above?

For the answer, read the next chapter about your super bio-computer chip, the Brain Cell.

brain workout

1. the evolving brain

To give yourself an even greater awareness of the importance of this point in human history for our evolving brain and brain knowledge, go back to page 15 and spend five or ten minutes noting down your own predictions for the next 10, 500, 10,000, 50,000, and 3 million years – the reverse, into the future, of the historical pyramid. This exercise is a wonderful game to play with your friends, and can result in entire evenings of fascinating conversation!

2. use both sides of your brain

Encourage yourself, like the great geniuses, to use "both sides of your brain." Review the different skills that your amazing cortex has, identify which ones are strong and which ones are weak, and then use the strong skills to develop the weak ones. In the remaining chapters of *Head Strong*, you will be introduced to many techniques to help you do this.

3. use your upper brain to control your lower brain

As Swami Rama did, begin to use your upper brain to control your lower brain. The simplest example of this is the "counting to 10" technique for calming yourself down when you are extremely angry.

Whenever you notice your temper getting out of control, use your cerebral cortex to make yourself take 10 deep breaths, during which time you consciously decide to take control of the situation yourself, rather than letting your emotions run roughshod over you!

4. learn to love your computer!

The fear that many people have of computers is understandable, though not necessary. Your brain can easily handle and outwit any computer. Consider the computer not so much as an enemy, but as a friendly pet that wants to help you – especially when you understand its limited-though-willing intelligence.

brain boosters

1. My brain is a masterpiece! I am increasingly understanding it and using it well.
2. In emotional situations I encourage my upper and lower brains to work in harmony to my best advantage.
3. I am developing the synergetic strength and power of the skills of my left and right cortex.
4. I am increasingly in awe of my brain and its incredible physical sophistication and its amazing mental powers.

answers to quick brain-check 4

1. False
2. False
3. False
4. False
5. True
6. True
7. True
8. True and False!
9. True and False!
10. False
11. False

chapter three

your super bio-computer chip: the brain cell

You are hard-wired for genius.

Tony Buzan

introduction

Now that you have a clear picture of the macroscopic, or "large picture" of the operations of your upper, lower, left, and right brains, you are about to embark upon an astounding adventure into the micro cosmos. On this adventure I will introduce you to the history of our knowledge concerning your personal amazing super-bio-computer chip – your brain cell.

I will teach you about its extraordinary capacities, the nature and structure of its body, the number of brain cells you have, the facts about brain cell loss, the way in which it functions independently, the way in which it functions with other brain cells, and the way in which your thoughts actually occur.

At the end of the chapter you will discover the structural differences between the brain cells of insects, animals and humans, and two enticing new facts about your thoughts – and about the probability of you having *any* thought.

quick brain-check 5 – brain cell literacy

Check out your mental literacy levels about your brain cell (answers on page 50)!

1. The number of brain cells in the human brain is:
   (a) 100,000?
   (b) 1 million?
   (c) 10 million?
   (d) 100 million?
   (e) 1 billion?
   (f) 1 trillion?

2. The brain of an insect like the bee contains millions of brain cells.   True/False?

3. The "population" of brain cells in your head is larger than the number of human beings on planet earth.   True/False?

4. We have been able to photograph a still picture of a brain cell, but have not yet been able to video a living brain cell.   True/False?

5. The great geniuses in history such as Leonardo da Vinci, Isaac Newton, Marie Curie and Albert Einstein probably reached their maximum potential.   True/False?

6. The average brain loses between 10,000 and 1 million brain cells per day.   True/False?

7. One standard measure of alcohol will cost you between 1,000 and 100,000 brain cells per slurp!   True/False?

8. The human brain can grow new connections between brain cells as it ages but cannot generate entirely new cells.   True/False?

9. The number of patterns of thought possible for your brain is
    equal to the number of atoms in:
    (a) A molecule?
    (b) A cathedral?
    (c) A mountain?
    (d) The moon?
    (e) The earth?
    (f) Our solar system including the sun?
    (g) Our galaxy and its 10 trillion stars?
    (h) None of these?

10. Repetition of a thought increases the probability of ....?

11. Thoughts are not "real" in the sense that the book you are
    reading is real.   True/False?

12. Note down all those different things you think a bee can do.

Now read on to find out the answers.

your brain cell – a history of our knowledge

For centuries the human brain had been considered merely as a three-and-a-half
pound structureless, characterless lump of gray matter. And then the intrigue
began. With the development of the microscope it was discovered that the
brain's crumpled outer layer was far more complex than had previously been
suspected. It was found that the brain was composed of thousands of intricate
and tiny rivers of blood that coursed throughout it, "feeding" the brain.

Next came the revolutionary and revelationary discovery that the brain seemed to
be composed of hundreds of thousands of tiny dots, the nature and function of which
remained a mystery for a while. Then, as the power of the microscope increased, it was
found that there were many more "dots" than previously had been thought, and that
each one appeared to have tiny extensions emanating from it. This launched a

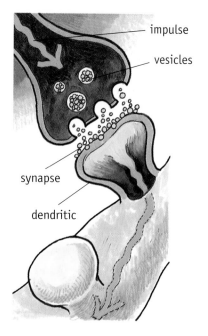

impulse

vesicles

synapse

dendritic

scientific saga similar to that of astronomy – in which the telescope and its discovery of the stars, solar systems, galaxies, and clusters of galaxies was the twin of the microscope and its penetration of the universes of your brain.

As the super-sensitive electron microscope appeared on the scene, it was discovered that each brain was composed of millions of tiny cells, called neurons. The body of each brain cell was found to be astoundingly complex, with a center, or nucleus, and a large number of branches radiating from it in all directions. The cells looked like beautifully complex trees that had been able to grow branches in all directions round it, and in three dimensions! (see Figure 5).

Figure 5: a brain cell and its connections

the number of your brain cells

The next stage in this *Star Trek*-like exploration of the microscopic universe was truly mind-boggling. In the last half of the 20th century, it was discovered that the number of brain cells was not just a few million – it was a *million* million! To appreciate the real value of this, rather than just thinking of it as another "very big number," think of it using both your "left brain" numerical skills and your "right brain" imagination and spatial skills. At the beginning of the 21st century the population of the world was estimated to be six billion people.

Number of brain cells: 1,000,000,000,000
Number of people: 6,000,000,000

The number of brain cells existing in your head is thus **166 times** the number of people on the planet!

You can imagine the excitement of the scientists when they discovered this, for it reflected the magnificence of their own brains as well...

The significance of this number would be immense, even if each brain cell could perform only very basic operations. If each brain cell were, however, immensely powerful, the significance of their number would take scientists into realms that are almost supernatural. In a very real sense you consciously lead, direct, nurture, and are responsible for the lives, activities and directions of a million million independent, intelligent beings – each one a genius! You are the equivalent of a Galactic Emperor!

Before we examine just how powerful each brain cell that you possess really is, let's dispel some dangerous misconceptions about loss of brain cells.

a global mind set

In the talks that I have given around the world during the last 30 years, I have asked thousands of audiences the following question: "What happens to your brain cells as you get older?"

Invariably people respond "they die!" (What surprises me is the almost *relish* with which people exclaim that fact!)

The next question, of course, is: "If this is so, then how many do you lose per day?"

The average estimate is between "thousands" and "millions."

Similarly, when people are asked "How many brain cells do you lose for every unit of alcohol taken?" the answer ranges between "a thousand" to "hundreds of thousands!"

Think, for a moment, of the global mind set that has been created, for *everyone* basically knows these depressing and disturbing "facts." Every morning billions of people wake up. The sun is shining, their true love is by their side, and there on the pillow are another million brain cells.

Have a nice day!

This realization causes a deep, global, melancholy: everyone knows that every day the central power-house of their intelligence, emotions, perceptions and being is losing its life-supplying and life-enhancing bio-computer chips by the thousands.

The natural reaction is to "batten down the hatches" and stick to whatever behavior patterns have proved relatively successful; to shy away from the giant army (or invading hordes) of up-and-coming younger brains who possess so much more brain cell equipment and armory!

Now for the Good News!

First, even if you *did* lose a million brain cells per day, it would still be relatively *insignificant* in relation to the vast number of brain cells you actually have. Look at the mathematics:

Number of days in the year	365
Pessimistic estimate of number of brain cells lost per day	1,000,000
Estimated loss in extended life span of 100 years	
(365 days x 1,000,000 per day)	36,500,000,000
Average number of brain cells	1,000,000,000,000
Estimated percentage of brain cells lost therefore in a 100	
year lifespan (36,500,000,000 ./. 1,000,000,000,000)	0.0365
Equals	**3.6 percent!**

Calculating from this figure the *yearly* loss, we come up with the even more insignificant figure of *0.36 of 1 percent per year* – utterly irrelevant, especially when you consider the power of the remaining 99.64 percent!

In addition, contrary to popular opinion, it has been found that a normal intake of two or three units of alcohol such as wine, especially with meals, causes *no* loss of brain cells. What apparently happens is that under the onslaught of alcohol, the brain cells seem to "cringe," drawing themselves in and "shrinking" in self-defence. Brain scans of alcoholics who had been "cold turkeyed" showed that their embattled brain cells had expanded back to near normal size, after they had "peeped out," seen that there was no danger on the horizon, and allowed their bodies to relax out to their normal, more expansive form.

There is *more* good news: all the above calculations were unnecessary, other than to make a point.

Why?

Because recent research has shown that in a normal, healthy brain (that is, one in a healthy, aerobically fit body in which the brain is used *well*) there is *no* apparent loss of brain cells; only a growth in the interconnections, and therefore multiple intelligences, of that brain!

And there is *even more* good news!

As the 20th century ended, biologists at Princeton University came up with the discovery that was named "the discovery of the year" (if not decade and century!) For the first time in history scientists discovered that parts of the human brain can generate thousands of *new* brain cells, *every day*.

Now that you are armed with the knowledge that you have a vast number of super bio-computer chips, that they don't die off, and that you are given a refreshingly new batch of a thousand or more every day, let's examine them.

brain cell power!

When investigating the power of the human brain cell, it is best first to analyze the brain capacity of an insect such as a bee. Why? Because, surprisingly, the bee (and every other living animal, including your common pets such as goldfish, rabbits, dogs, and cats) has exactly the same super-bio-computer chip as you and I. That is why so many people feel such exceptional levels of communication with their pets – it is because they are looking at each other with brains that are based on the same fundamental unit of construction.

As with our own brains, we are discovering that animal brains are far more complex and powerful than we had previously thought, and that the animal kingdom is composed of far more geniuses than we had thought!

If the bee's tiny, miniature brain is composed of the same basic bio-computer chips as ours, we can get a very clear picture of the power of one bio-computer chip by analyzing the brain capacity of that tiny insect. How many brain cells does the bee have in order to "manufacture" all its behaviors? Not the few million that many people expect, but a mere few thousand.

Assuming that a given bee has 10,000 brain cells, let's compare that as a percentage to the number we have.

Number of bee brain cells	10,000
Number of human brain cells	1,000,000,000,000
Percentage of bee brain cells to human brain cells	1/100,000,000
Equals	**0.000001 percent!**

With those few thousand brain cells, that 100-millionth of our own brain cell volume, what can a bee do? (See your own answers to this question posed on page 31.)

the bee game

what can a bee do?

With their few thousand brain cells bees can:

1. **Build** Bees are among the master architects of the insect world, constructing intricate and complex "high-rises" that can house entire communities.
2. **Care** for their young.
3. **Collect** pollen and information.
4. **Communicate** By movement, sound and gesture, bees can communicate to others intricate information concerning plant locations and types of blossom.
5. **Count** Bees can locate chosen objects again by remembering the number of significant items on the way to the desired goal.

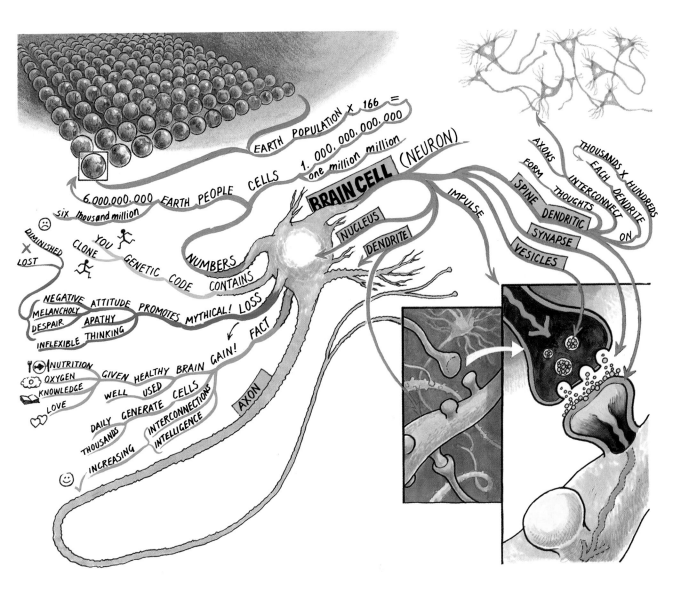

EARTH POPULATION X 166 = 1.000.000.000.000 one million million

BRAIN CELL (NEURON)

6.000.000.000 EARTH PEOPLE CELLS
six thousand million

NUMBERS CONTAINS

DIMINISHED
LOST
CLONE YOU GENETIC CODE

NEGATIVE ATTITUDE PROMOTES MYTHICAL! LOSS
MELANCHOLY
DESPAIR APATHY
INFLEXIBLE THINKING
FACT

NUTRITION
OXYGEN
KNOWLEDGE
LOVE
GIVEN HEALTHY BRAIN GAIN!
WELL USED CELLS
DAILY GENERATE INTERCONNECTIONS
THOUSANDS INTELLIGENCE
INCREASING

AXON

NUCLEUS
DENDRITE
IMPULSE

AXONS
FORM
SPINE
DENDRITIC
SYNAPSE
VESICLES
THOUSANDS X HUNDREDS
EACH DENDRITE
INTERCONNECT
THOUGHTS
ON

Mind Map® 5

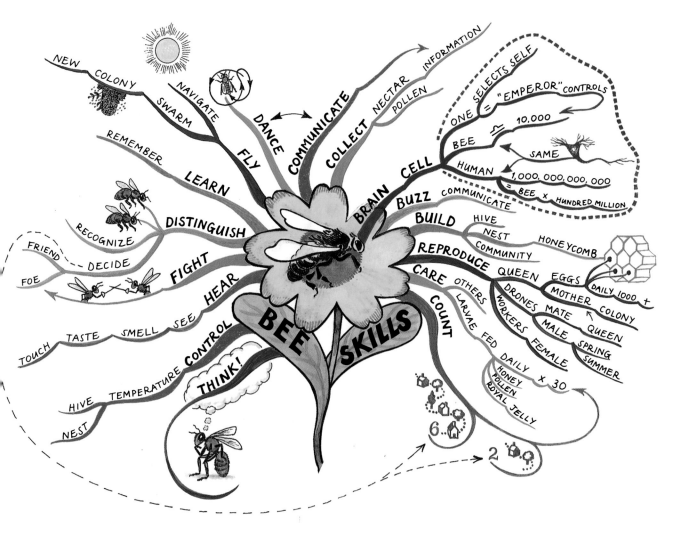

6. **Dance** When bees return to the hive they perform a complex dance that conveys to their companions the location and navigational information about a new find.

7. **Distinguish** other bees.

8. **Eat.**

9. **Fight** Not only fight, but fight with such ferocity, focus, speed and coordination of its multiple fighting appendages, that it makes even speeded-up karate films look slow and pathetic by comparison.

10. **Fly** Just imagine what those few thousand brain cells have to do to accomplish this!

11. **Hear** Just like us.

12. **Learn** See points 4 and 5 above.

13. **Live** in an organized community and function appropriately (compare our own behavior!)

14. **Make decisions.** Bees can decide to change the temperature of their hive, to convey or not convey information, to fight and to migrate.

15. **Navigate** On a miniature scale, the bee is the equivalent of any of our most sophisticated aircraft. Imagine trying to land (which a bee can) on a waving leaf in a strong and gusting wind.

16. **Produce honey.**

17. **Regulate temperature** When the hive becomes too hot, a group of bees will work in harmony to "reset" the temperature of the hive to within one-tenth of a degree centigrade, using their wings as a giant communal fan, and beating cool air through the hive until the desired temperature is reached.

18. **Remember** They could not count, communicate or survive if they didn't!

19. **Reproduce.**

20. **See** including ultraviolet light.

21. **Smell.**

22. **Swarm** in more intricate formation than jet fighter squadrons.

23. **Taste.**

24. **Think.**
25. **Touch.**

Entomological research has recently discovered that one of the bee's brain cells, more or less randomly, decides to become the "Emperor Brain Cell." Although in structure and composition it is identical to all the other brain cells, it simply decides that it will take over the general monitoring and direction of the entire system. It therefore appears that one single brain cell can actually mastermind all the activities of this amazing insect's amazing brain!

If a bee can do all this with its few *thousand* brain cells, are we making the most of our *million, million* cells?! Probably not!

For those readers who are teachers, parents, or who are in any way involved with children, the Bee Game is a wonderful game to play with them. When children realize what the individual brain cell can do, and when they realize the enormity of the little bee's accomplishments, they immediately gain a new appreciation for nature, and a newly developed sense of their own self-worth.

a million million yous

In addition to the skills noted above, each one of your million, million brain cells contains the exact genetic code to clone you – to produce an identical physical replica of you. Thus the illustration of 166-planets-worth of six billion human beings is even more appropriate, for within your brain cells that potential actually exists!

your brain cell and the computer

By now it should be becoming apparent to you that your average brain cell dwarfs the capacity of the average personal computer, and the answer to the Quick Brain-Check question on page 25 is in fact (i), "bigger than *all* the above!" In fact, if we were to represent the strength and power of the world's greatest

super-computer by that two-storey house, the potential power of your own brain would be represented by a building far bigger than the 100-storey skyscraper. The strength and power of your own brain would be represented by a heaven-scraper 10 blocks square at the base and reaching to the moon! As we said, allow your brain to treat the computer as the friendly little willing-to-help pet that it really is.

So, now, think of the true potential of your brain. It is composed not only of a million million super-bio-computer chips – those super-bio-computer chips are super-bio-computers themselves! In your brain they are linked in multiple parallel ways that produce mathematics about you even more staggering than the giant numbers at which we have so far been looking.

Let's look next at what the microscopic voyagers further discovered on their journey into the intricacies of the body of your brain cell.

the intricate structure of brain cells

With more powerful instruments, the electron-microscopists discovered that each one of the thousands of branches on each brain cell itself contained its own extensions. These extensions were like little mushrooms. As the electron-microscopes became more powerful and delved ever deeper into the mysteries of the brain cell, we discovered that each of these little buttons, as we had discovered with the original "little dots" in the cortex, contained its own astounding universe.

Within each button there were hundreds of thousands - millions – of tiny vesicles, each containing a specially coded bundle of chemicals waiting to be activated (see Figure 5, page 32).

In the same way, the cell's nucleus appeared to be much more than simply "the center of the brain cell." It was, rather, the brain cell's own "brain" and, based on what we know about the bee, a tiny brain of magnificent power. Literally, a brain within a brain, within your brain!

And then, at the end of the 20th century, the next miraculous discovery was made. The Max Planck Laboratory filmed, for the first time in human history, a *living* brain cell. It had been taken from a living brain and was contained in a deep rectangular channel of brain fluid in a petri dish under the electron-microscope. The film, which has changed the lives of all those who have seen it, showed this amazing little being to have a completely independent intelligence. With its hundreds of baby-like hands, like an amoeba, it extended and retracted, sensitively and focusedly reaching out to every atom of the space in its newly confined universe – looking for connection. It was like seeing the most impossibly delicate, sensitive and intelligent being from outer space.

brain cell thoughts

When people from around the world were asked to note down what words came to mind while they were watching this remarkable little intelligence on film, the following were the most common:

Ability	Beautiful
Active	Communication
Adaptable	Creativity
Adventurous	Curious
Amazing	Disciplined
Astonishing	Dynamic
Awesome	Exploratory

Extraordinary	Radiant
Fantastic	Searching
Fascinating	Systematic
Genius	Tireless
Incredible	Unique
Intelligent	Universal
Magical	Unstoppable
Moving	Vibrant
Persistent	Wonderful
Playful	Wondrous
Potential	Wow!
Powerful	

Standing in awe watching this tiny little entity, the human beings viewing it were marking a turning point in human evolution. They were among the first humans to witness living intelligence: they were the first Intelligences to observe Intelligence in Action. What is remarkable and heart-warming is that these responses came from people of all different ages, races, nations, educational levels and demographic levels, and they were identical. Everyone was in awe and amazed by the magnificence of what they were seeing.

The extraordinary compilation of words you have just read was used by human beings to describe, perhaps without consciously being aware of it, *themselves*.

You!

Us!

What they shared, in addition to the common reaction and identical appreciation, was the identical unit of intelligence that had so stunned them with its awesome power and beauty.

(Remember that these words apply to *you*, and think of them especially when you are reading about and practicing **Meta-Positive Thinking** in Chapter 4.)

How, then, does each one of these amazing brain cell creatures relate to others?

the brain cell and its friends

Your brain cell operates by forming fantastically complex links with tens of thousands of its neighbors and companions. These links are made primarily when its main and biggest branch (the axon) makes multiple thousands of connections with the little buttons on many thousands of many branches of many thousand other brain cells. (See Figure 5, page 32.)

Each contact point is known as a synapse. When an electro-magnetic bio-chemical message (the nerve impulse) surges down the axon, it is released through the synaptic button, which is connected to the dendritic spine. Between the two there is a tiny space.

The nerve impulse fires hundreds of thousands of the spheres called vesicles across the synaptic gap in what, in the microcosmic world, must look like a mega Niagara Falls. These vesicles journey at lightning speed across the synaptic gap and attach, like millions of messenger pigeons, to the surface of the dendritic spine. The messages are then transmitted along the branches of the receiving brain cell to its own axon, which then transmits the message through its branches to other brain cells, and so on and on and on, creating the intricate pathway of a thought.

Now knowing the incredible physical, biological, and chemical complexity of just one of the billions of thoughts you have every day, you can understand why it so important that your brain is fed with a five-star diet of nutrition, oxygen, information, and affection.

For the first time in the history of humankind, advanced imaging technology lets you watch a living human brain think a thought. Seeing your brain in action not only gives you a much deeper appreciation for how smart a human-being can be, it also reveals why it is so important to learn correctly.

Networker Magazine, Jan/Feb 1999

brain principle number 2 – the knowledge-seeking brain

We now reach the second of our **Brain Principles** – the brain is a **Knowledge-**seeking mechanism. In fact, as you have just learned, information is one of the prerequisites for the brain and brain cells to survive. As you can see from the way your brain cells operate, they require a constant diet of data/knowledge in order to keep them activated – in order to give them a reason and purpose for using the nutritional and oxygen energy sources which we will look at in Chapters 7 and 8.

How much knowledge can your brain store? As you know from the number of physical permutations and combinations of the brain cells' thinking capacity, it is an infinite amount.

Combine this with the **Synergy Principle** (see page 4), and your knowledge of how your brain cells relate to each other, and you will see that it is necessary to make sure that your knowledge source is correct and that data is dealt with in appropriately synergetic ways. If you do this, your brain and body thinking will improve, your possibilities for new brain and body thinking will improve, and your brain and body thinking about possibilities will improve! (See Figure 7.) I will cover ways of guaranteeing that your knowledge acquisition is appropriate in the next chapter.

Each pattern of thought is known as a memory trace (literally a "track" of memory) or a thought map. It is also, very significantly, a *habit*. Even more significantly, it is a physical actuality – an "engineering" fact, a biological reality. Your thoughts are REAL.

The only limiting factor, biologically, to the number of thoughts, memories, behavior patterns and habits that are available to you must lie in the physical limitation of the pattern-making potential of your amazing brain.

With a million, million brain cells, many with hundreds of

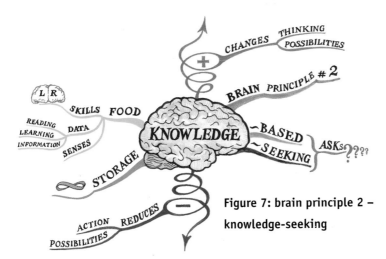

Figure 7: brain principle 2 – knowledge-seeking

thousands of branches, each branch with hundreds of thousands of connection points, each with trillions of messengers, and each connection point capable of forming billions upon billions of different patterns, the number must be gigantic. In fact, by the middle of the last century the number had already been established at one followed by one hundred zeros – a number of astronomical proportions.

This number turned out to be wrong, too small and in need of revision. If the revised number had simply been to add one zero it would have been an astronomical increase. The *actual* revised number added *seven hundred* zeros – in other words the number became one followed by eight hundred zeros! To put this in context, this number represents the number of atoms in the local universe.

Professor Anokhin, the great psychologist Pavlov's most brilliant pupil, who himself became the top brain scientist in Russia, worked on this matter for a number of years, and came up with a number that revised even the giant eight hundred zeros number. He calculated that your brain has a pattern-making potential not of one followed by a hundred zeros, nor one followed by eight hundred zeros, but one followed by ten-and-a-half-million *kilometers* of standard type-written zeros!! This would cover a piece of paper long enough to go to the moon and back *14* times!

Anokhin then went on to say that, biologically and mechanically, no one, not even the greatest geniuses, had come even near to using the fundamental potential of the human brain. He declared it to be infinite.

new thought about thought and new thought

The next great discovery about the magical Merlin-like brain cell and its patterns of thinking, was that repetition of a thought decreases the biochemical resistance to that thought happening again.

A good metaphor here is that of a virgin jungle. Imagine that you are armed with a machete and that you have to fight your way through from one side to another. The first time you go through (the first time you have that thought) there would be lots of resistance to your passage. If, the minute you had reached the other side, you were lifted up by helicopter and placed once again at the starting point, and asked to go through the jungle again, you would encounter, what? Obviously slightly less resistance, because of the pathway you had already made. Every time you went through, you would make the pathway a little larger, and the resistance to your passageway would be a little less each time. If you and others continued to use the pathway, it would eventually become a track, then a small road, then a larger road, and eventually a major highway.

So it is with your brain. Every time you think a thought, the resistance to it is reduced.

This extremely significant fact leads to one that is even *more* so in terms of understanding your behavior, learning, habits and the general development of your potential.

quick brain-check 6 – probabilities of thoughts

If repetition of a thought reduces resistance, then that same repetition must increase the probability of something in turn. The probability of what?! Quickly jot down your thought/s.

The most common responses to this question are:

- Memory
- Learning
- Success
- Improvement
- Creativity
- Intelligence
- Growth
- Mental Power

The response to each of those answers is "maybe," "maybe," "maybe," "maybe,"...

Try this: what does practice make?...

"Perfect!" is the normal (habitual!) reply.

But *does* practice make perfect? Supposing you practice the wrong thing?

There is *one* thing that the repetition of a thought increases the probability of:

The repetition of a thought increases the probability of ... REPETITION!

Everything you do or say or think or feel increases the probability that you will do, say, think, or feel in the same way again. If you do things well, speak and think positively, and generally feel good about yourself, others, the world and the universe, the probability continually increases that you will do better, talk and think better, and feel and be better. And you have an infinite capacity to do and to be so. And it is *REAL*.

However, if (and herein is concealed the lurking mental monster), you do poorly, think and act negatively, practice inadequately, and regularly feel bad about yourself, others, the world and the universe, then with *every* such thought and act you increase the probability of a continuing and deepening downward spiral. Negative thought patterns are *real*, and your capacity to create them is *infinite*.

An infinitely positive and optimistic futurescape, or an infinitely negative futurescape? The choice is yours, and the *natural* choice of your astounding brain is for the *positive* scenario. It is only when the brain receives incorrect data and inappropriate formulas that it, unnaturally, gets caught up in the downward spiral (see **Synergy Brain Principle**, page 4).

Our new understanding of the brain and its mysteries has allowed us to unlock the correct formula for appropriate-brain-thinking. As you would expect, these new insights are based on the information you have just read about the incredible brain cell. They go well beyond traditional positive-thinking techniques, and take you into the enchanting world of **Meta-Positive Thinking**.

This forms the basis of the next chapter, and launches you into Part II of *Head Strong*.

brain cell workout

1. look after your brain cells!

Now that you know just how incredibly intricate and intelligent each one of your million million brain cells is, commit yourself even more strongly to looking after and nurturing them to the best of your ability. As you read the following chapters, actively hunt for information that will help you help your brain cells.

2. rejoice in your brain cells!

Spread the good news to your family and friends about the brain cell statistics – about the million million each of us have; about the fact that we *don't* necessarily lose brain cells; and about the fact that we apparently gain a fresh supply of a minimum of a thousand a day!

3. remember your own brain-power

Remember the bee. Every time you see (or hear!) a bee, remember the Bee Game. Use your upper brain to reflect for a moment on how magnificent that little intelligence is. Then contemplate your own potential again. Use your lower brain to feel the awe-emotions that arise.

Play the Bee Game with children whenever you can.

4. choose your favorite brain cell thoughts from pages 42–3.

Place them in your home/study/place of work where you can use them as a constant reminder of just how magnificent and amazing you are. In the next chapter you will discover more about just how important it is to review constantly these words, and the extraordinarily positive effects they will have on you if you do.

5. remember the magic formula

"Repetition increases the probability of repetition."

brain boosters

1. I have a million million brain cells. Each one is a mini-genius. I am their commander and am committed to lead them well.
2. My brain is millions of times more powerful than the world's most powerful computer.
3. I enjoy treating computers as useful friends.
4. As repetition increases the probability of repetition, I will feed my brain a diet of healthy and positive thoughts.
5. I am a/an .... human being. (Fill in your favorite five brain cell thoughts.)

answers to quick brain-check 5

1. (f)
2. False – they contain only a few thousand
3. True
4. False
5. False
6. False
7. False
8. False
9. (i)! – it is far greater than any of the previous possible answers
10. Repetition
11. False

brain and body thinking skills

meta-positive thinking
creative & radiant thinking

4

chapter four

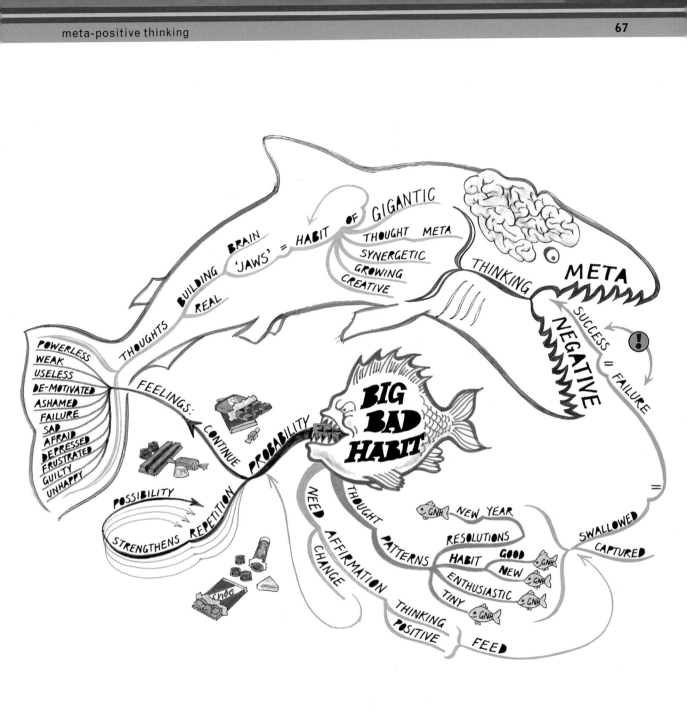

Mind Map® 7

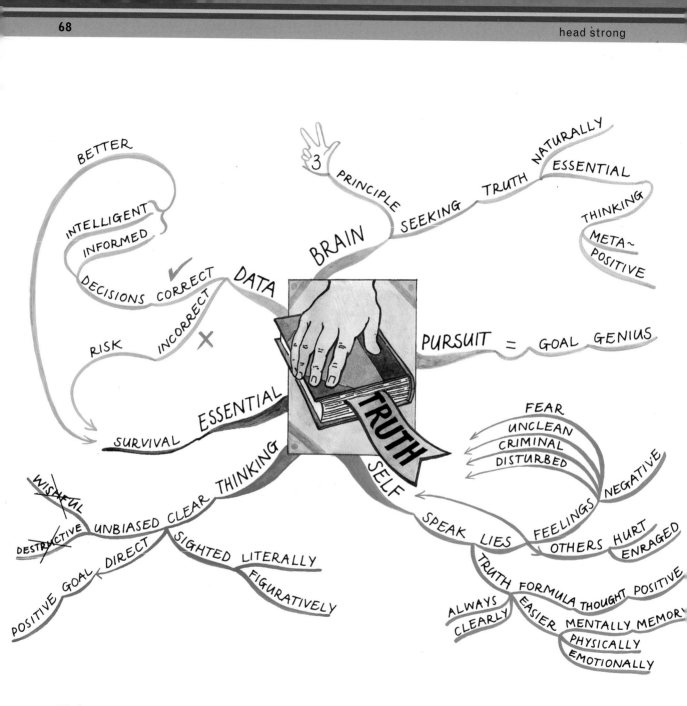

Mind Map® 8

If you want to amuse and educate yourself in this particular aspect of **Meta-Positive Thinking**, read the sports pages of the newspapers, and notice how many national and world-level coaches and athletes regularly make the "Negative Goal" mistake, simply because they haven't learned about the internal mechanics and thinking processes of their brains.

Remember – in **Meta-Positive Thinking** you must always direct your mind to a vision (a clear image) that is positive.

numbers 7–11

These five affirmations are also all inappropriate and although some have more than one fault, these five all share one fault in common. Can you spot it? Go back and check...

What they share in common is that they are all *lies*! I don't hate chocolates – I love them almost better than anything! I don't like being fat. I am not thin, and I am not healthy.

This means that if I repeat these affirmations on a daily basis, I will also be building up another horrible thought pattern, which is: "I am a liar; I am a liar; I am dishonest; I am a liar ..."

With this growing realization building like a pustule in my brain, how will I feel? Torn, morally unclean, untruthful, criminal, and afraid. And in such a disturbed and upsetting mental state, what will I need to comfort me? CHOCOLATES!

Tony rises to 306 pounds...

brain principle number 3 – truth

Beholding the bright countenance of truth in the quiet and still air of delightful studies.

John Milton

Time's glory is to calm contending kings,
to unmask falsehood and bring truth to light.

William Shakespeare

The Third **Brain Principle** is an important and encouraging one. It states, quite simply, that your brain is a **Truth**-seeking mechanism. Why? Because the gathering of Truth is fundamentally a survival mechanism for your brain. If you have incorrect data about the world around you, the decisions you make based on that incorrect data will put your life at risk. Conversely, if you have correct (true) data, your brain will make more intelligent and informed decisions, and your chances of survival will be greater. It is interesting to note that many of the greatest geniuses stated that their fundamental life's goal was the pursuit of Truth.

I have three friends, Socrates, Aristotle and the Truth.

Isaac Newton

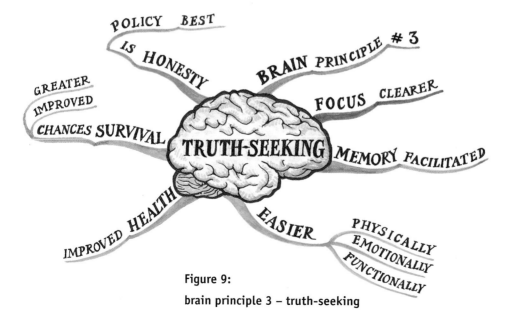

Figure 9:
brain principle 3 – truth-seeking

If you don't the know the Truth about the relationships between, for example, a relatively static human and a hurtling five-ton lorry, then your observation of that lorry might be the last piece of information your brain ever receives!

The **Truth Brain Principle** explains why all people, and especially children, will put up with astonishing levels of discomfort, inconvenience and bad behavior, but will always be hurt or enraged if they are lied to.

When you are speaking to yourself you need to tell the Truth as often and as clearly as you can. This is especially important in **Meta-Positive Thinking**, as you are repeating your thoughts many times a day and thousands of times a year.

numbers 12–16

Like numbers 7–11, affirmations 12–16 contain one common fault. Go back to page 59 and see if you can spot it.

Affirmations 12–16 share the common trait of all being horrifyingly *negative* in the images that they are placing in my brain. Think of it: every day I will be reminding myself, several times a day, about being fatter, dying, having more spots, of images of human excrement, sickness, vomiting, pain, constipation, and loneliness. In addition to all that, I will be reminding myself that my sex life will increasingly be in ruins!

Unfortunately, negative Positive Thinking approaches are prevalent at the moment. All over the world hundreds of millions of people are trying to make their lives more happy, beautiful and successful by transforming their brains, unwittingly, into rubbish tips.

So, returning to 306-pound Tony, how will I feel, thinking about such things every day? Repulsed, depressed, inadequate, and alone. And what will I need to do to help me get over these horrible feelings? Eat CHOCOLATES!!

Tony has now gone to 308 pounds...

The thoughts in **Meta-Positive Thinking** *must* be *attractive* to your brain. The very word "attractive" explains why – if the thoughts are attractive, then your brain will be *attracted* to them. Unpleasant thoughts will make your brain want to shy away from them, and will create unnecessary tension and stress in your body.

An interesting variation on this negative theme is the approach of stuffing yourself with chocolates to make you sick, thus creating negative associations with chocolates that would supposedly stop the habit.

This "aversion therapy" seldom, if ever, works.

The **MNTH** Brain simply refers to its history books, and notes that the Romans perfected the art of gorging and then enforcing vomiting, for the sheer pleasure of emptying the stomach in order that they could continue to eat what they loved. In my case, what I love is chocolates, so this technique will actually have me consuming more!

numbers 17–20

Unfortunately none of these work either. They all share the common fault of not being particularly *relevant* to the situation. For example, "small is beautiful" may well be true, but so what? Middling can also be beautiful, and so can large. And if I keep repeating to myself that "small is beautiful," I will expand my chocolate research and eating into the delicious universe of small chocolates, which I will add to my smorgasbord!

Tony is now 310 pounds and rising...

Your affirmation must be *relevant* to the situation you are addressing.

numbers 21–23

These three look as if they might be satisfactory. They are not! They contain within them a subtly hidden goal that can become very dangerous, and that has indeed led to the deaths of thousands of people. Is our mutual goal for me simply for me to lose weight and be thin? No. I can lose weight by chopping off a limb or by starvation. Losing weight is, to coin a phrase, too "thin" a goal for the **Meta-Positive Thinker**. And it can, as I have said, have dangerous repercussions.

The international fashion-industry campaign to convince women (and, increasingly, men too) that they should be thin succeeds in many tragic cases. A girl stands in front of the mirror with the affirmation *"You should be thinner, you should be thinner, you should be thinner, you should be thinner ..."* ricocheting around her brain, and growing in strength as a Very **Big Bad Habit**. What therefore does she see each time she looks in the mirror, no matter how thin she is? Excess fat. And what must she do? Her brain is consistently telling her to "get *thinner*." And so on it goes until the power-house of her brain has reduced her body to a skeleton.

The condition is *anorexia nervosa*, and I suggest that the reason why so many anorexics, and the people who try to help them, have such a mighty (and sadly often losing) battle is not so much for standard "psychological" reasons. It can be traced to a growing **Big Bad Habit** that reinforces **Meta-Negative Thinking**, which is itself reinforced every day by great swathes of society and by the victims themselves, thus creating an ever-increasing probability that the victims will self-destruct.

When creating your own **Meta-Positive Thinking Formula**, be aware that this danger exists, and sculpt your affirmations to be *truly* positive and directed to your overall benefit.

numbers 24–26

Like the previous three, these affirmations sound as if they might be useful. Like the previous three, they are not! For example, consider "I can choose what to do." Of course you can. But so what? This self-evident truth does not add anything to your existing store of knowledge, and gives you no direction. On top of which, it gives you total freedom to choose what to do. Similarly for your poor friend Tony – what is he probably going to choose to do? Eat CHOCOLATES!!

Tony balloons to 312 pounds...

The common fault they share is that they provide no commands to action; no *motive*. A good **Meta-Positive Thinking** affirmation must give you impetus and must be *proactive*.

numbers 27–29

Are *these*, then, the correct ones?

No! They each contain a subtle error which will inevitably lead to failure. Go back to page 63 and see if you can spot it.

Of course I want to be more attractive and I want to be healthy. And I want a million dollars. And I want the environment to be safe. And I want a private jet. And I want and I want and I want and I want.

The fault that these three share is that they are *wishful* thinking. Wishful thinking is simply that: *thinking* about your wishes. Once again it gives you no motive, no direction, and by its constant repetition in your brain it makes the probability that you will wish again greater, the probability that you will do anything about it ever *smaller*, and the probability that you will become increasingly frustrated and disillusioned *even* greater. Wishful thinking, which has your head going round and round in useless circles, never reaching its goal, is much like the dog chasing its tail.

In such a situation I am sure that both you and I would add to our wish list, *what*? Another box of CHOCOLATES!!

Tony continues to balloon – to 314 pounds...

numbers 30–35

This group of affirmations is one of the most popular in the positive-thinking schools, and could well contain the answer.

Does it?

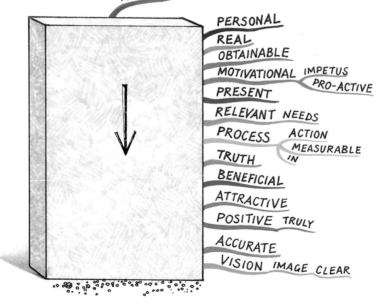

REPEATED

PERSONAL
REAL
OBTAINABLE
MOTIVATIONAL IMPETUS
                    PRO-ACTIVE
PRESENT
RELEVANT NEEDS
PROCESS ACTION
              MEASURABLE
TRUTH   IN
BENEFICIAL
ATTRACTIVE
POSITIVE TRULY
ACCURATE
VISION IMAGE CLEAR

Figure 10: the meta-positive thinking formula

Yes! ... And No!

"Yes," in that these affirmations lead us to a penultimate and important fact about what must be included in our **Meta-Positive Thinking Formula**. "No," in that they contain the most subtle and invidious error of thinking – an error that has led millions of well-intentioned, intelligent and directed people into years of frustration and apparently inexplicable failure. Think about what all these affirmations say: they say "I will; I will; I will; I will."

In so saying they lead the brain into an ultimately clever and almost invisible trap. For the brain has been duped into saying that it will improve. And when is this? In the future! And what can the genius **Big Bad Habit** and **Meta-Negative Thinking** do in between now and the time when "I will?" Have another box of CHOCOLATES!!

And when I have eaten that box of chocolates, have further ballooned to 316 pounds, and am feeling nicely Meta-Negatively useless, fat, and horrible, what will I do to help myself? Repeat my affirmation "I will ... ," once again unwittingly pushing my goal into the future, and once again giving me the opportunity and freedom to do what? Have another box of CHOCOLATES!!

Tony has now bloated to 318 pounds, and rising...

What does this mean in terms of our **Meta-Positive Thinking Formula**? It is obvious that we cannot phrase the affirmation in the past tense, as this would give us no direction at all, and would simply reconfirm historical information. We have just discovered that projecting affirmations into the future leads us into an eternal "tomorrow and tomorrow and tomorrow" of putting off action. This leaves us with only once choice: *affirmations must be made in the present tense.*

Even though I am now 318 pounds, we are nearly there!

number 36

Is this the ultimate answer? Many people think that it is, and this form of "positive thinking" has become widespread. Tempting as it may seem, this affirmation is the ultimate disaster! Think about what is going on from your brain cells' and habit-growing points of view.

We have me standing naked in front of my mirror, looking at 318 pounds of untrained, unfit adipose tissue, every ounce of which is me! Looking at them with what? My eyes, each of which contains 130 *million* light receivers. Each light receiver takes in billions of photons of sight-information per second, and every single photon and every single light receiver is confirming the objective fact that that thing in the mirror is me. And what am I saying as I observe this **Truth**? "That is *not* me!"

What I am thus telling my brain, with every repetition of my affirmation, is not only that that is not me, but also, by definition, that my eyes are lying. I am therefore building in my brain another giant habit, which is built on the unconscious repetition of the thought *"My eyes lie – what they see is not real; my eyes lie – what they see is not real; my eyes lie – what they see is not real."*

People who use such an affirmation have often been found gradually to lose visual contact with reality and others, constantly averting their eyes, and never clearly focusing on any external reality.

In addition to which, if that creature in the mirror is not me, and I am really lithe, fit, sexy, and strong, what can I do with no repercussions at all? Eat more CHOCOLATES!!

Next time, when I come back and look again in the mirror at the 320-pound Tony

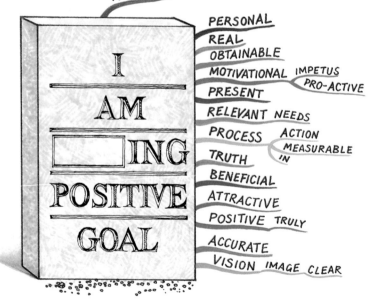

Figure 11: meta-positive thinking – the ultimate formula

Buzan, I will confirm that that even larger version of myself is not me *either*, that I am still the magnificent and attractive athlete I am saying (that is, lying!) I am, and I will therefore be able to eat even more CHOCOLATES!!

Tony is now 322 pounds and needs immediate rescue!

•   •   •

You now have all the information you need to rescue me.

meta-positive thinking – the ultimate formula

The **Big Bad Habit** and **Meta-Negative Thinking Habit** are nearly surrounded! Let's now fill in the final missing pieces of the jigsaw. We know that the affirmation must be *personal*, because "I" am speaking to myself. We know that it must be in the *present tense*, so I must say "I am ... " and we know that I must also direct myself to a *positive goal* while telling the truth. So we now have:

"I am '------' ('------' is a positive goal)."

In the example we are using in this chapter, what is my positive goal? Is it to be thin? No. We have already decided that is a dangerous vision. We also know that it is not to stop eating chocolates, for that will simply increase the strength of the habit. The underlying positive goal is to be *healthy* – healthy in body (and in mind), and to have all the benefits that that health will bring. These will include better poise, more stamina, a more toned and muscular body, more flexibility, and more vigor. With such a goal the loss of weight will be incidental, being the result of the larger, more complete and more *beneficial* vision of health. The idea of health is also a *real* and *obtainable* goal – two other qualities that are essential in **Meta-Positive Thinking**.

So, can we say "I am healthy?" Obviously not, because that is now even more of a lie than it was at the start of this Brain Game!

So what is this final missing piece that will surround the **BBHs** and **MNTH**, and which will set the brain free on an infinite journey of self-improvement?

What do you think a fitting word or phrase should be, or the kind of word or phrase it should be?

The word or phrase must be a PROCESS word or phrase, which includes the concept of *action*, which is *measurable*, and which forces your brain to *be in* that process. My final **Meta-Positive Thinking** affirmation will therefore be any one of the following:

- "I am *becoming* healthy."
- "I am *becoming* healthier."
- "I am *in the process of* becoming healthier."
- "I am *getting* more and more healthy."
- "I am *getting* healthier."

a good new habit

Now look at what happens in the brain and to the thought patterns when I repeat, five times a day or more, day after day, "I am becoming healthier" or "I am in the process of becoming healthier." Is there any way the **Meta-Negative Thinking Habit Brain** can escape?

No!

It is caught in the present, it is committed to the truth, it is forced toward a *positive goal*, and it is increasingly *directing* itself toward the *process* and *vision* of *becoming healthier*. No matter how much the **Big Bad Habits** and the **Meta-Negative Thinking Habits** struggle, this **Good New Habit** will survive, and will continue to grow with every repetition, thus constantly increasing the

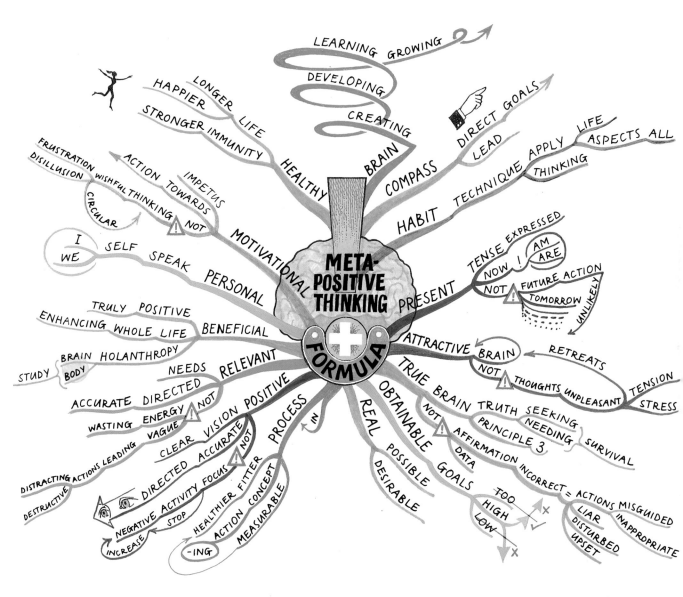

Mind Map® 9

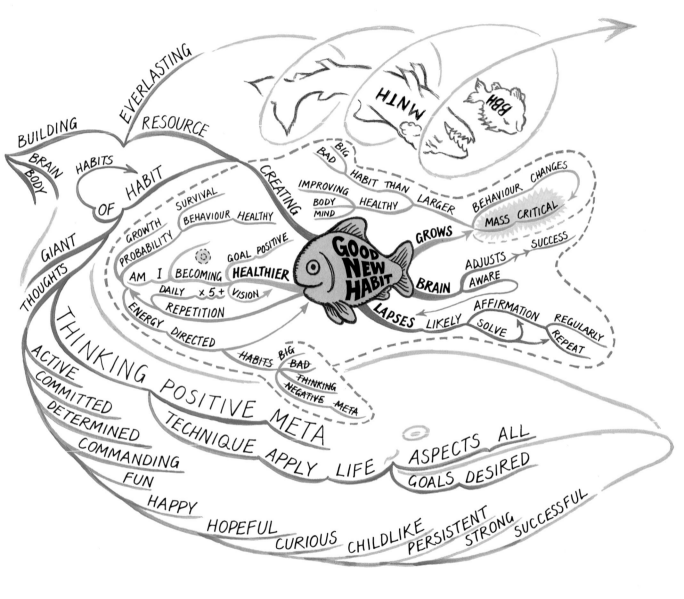

Mind Map® 10

probability that behavior will become directed toward health. None of the pitfalls of other "positive thinking" formulas are included in the **Meta-Positive Thinking Formula**, and so, as the **Good New Habit** grows and grows, no additional strength or energy is supplied to the **Big Bad Habit** and the **Meta-Negative Thinking Habit**.

At certain stages of your progression, your **Big Bad Habits** and **Meta-Negative Thinking Habits** will gain the upper hand. This is as it should be, for your **Good New Habit** is still young and very small. Always bear in mind as you continue to repeat your affirmation, that *Repetition increases the probability of Repetition*. Even when you think you might be "losing the battle," remember that every repetition helps your **Good New Habit** to grow, and increases the probability of your goal being achieved.

In the first few days and weeks of its growth, the **Good New Habit** will obviously remain tiny in comparison to the **Big Bad Habit**. Will I therefore eat more chocolates? Of course I will. As I do, and as the **Good New Habit** grows, my brain will be aware of the fact that I am eating chocolates as I am in the process of becoming healthier. It will therefore *adjust*, perhaps slightly shifting my regular diet to a more healthy one, perhaps taking me out for slightly longer walks, or perhaps having me join a health club.

As time progresses, and as my **Good New Habit** grows and grows in size and power, my behavior will continue to change, until one magical day when the **Good New Habit** reaches critical mass and becomes larger than the **Big Bad Habit**. At this point I will be truly healthy in both body and mind. If I continue the affirmation, I will continue to improve my health.

Sometimes you will hear of people who have "suddenly changed." Common examples include those who change from being completely messy and disorganized to being almost militarily neat and orderly, and those who change from being sullen, withdrawn and unfriendly to being happy and outgoing. Be assured that these changes were *not* sudden. These individuals had been working on themselves in many different ways, and the "sudden change" was that moment when the **Good New Habit** reached critical mass.

meta-positive thinking

While I have been building my **Good New Habit**, I will have been creating something even more interesting and even more profoundly valuable to me – the **Meta-Positive Thinking Habit**.

In the same way that my **Big Bad Habit** gave rise to **Meta-Negative Thinking**, so the **GNH** will give rise to its own giant thinking habit.

This habit is the opposite of the **Meta-Negative Habit**, and like the **Meta-Negative Thinking Habit** is a **Habit of Habits** – a **Habit of all the Good Thinking Habits: Meta-Positive Thinking**.

Words that describe the Meta-Positive Thinker include the following:

- Active
- Committed
- Determined
- Fun
- Happy
- Hopeful
- In control
- Open
- Optimistic
- Persistent
- Strong
- Successful

The **Meta-Positive Thinking Habit** is like a magic goldmine. The more you mine it, the more gold it possesses! It is both a thinking technique that you can apply to any aspect of your life, as well as a compass that will lead you to all of your desired goals. The words that describe *it* can be the words that describe *you*, as above.

Research is increasingly showing that these positive frames of mind *alone* can produce a stronger immune system and an all-round more healthy body;

they also extend your life span. (See Chapters 7 and 8 for more on this.) It is also a nicer life to live!

think yourself fit

Research results announced in 1998 at Manchester Metropolitan University in England by Dave Smith and his colleagues showed that the brain is so powerful that it can actually "*think itself fit*."

A group of 18 volunteers were asked to do a muscular pushing exercise. They were divided into three sub-groups. Six were asked to repeat the exercise twice a week for a month. Six had to imagine, very strongly, doing the workouts, but never actually to do them. Six were asked to do nothing at all during the same time period (but not with the same frequency!)

The results showed that the group which actually did the physical exercise increased their push-strength by 33 percent.

The group that did nothing showed no performance improvement.

The group that merely imagined doing the exercise increased their performance by *16 percent*.

Professor Smith commented:

"It's due not to what's happening in the muscle, but in the brain. If you can improve the neural input to the muscle, you can recruit more muscle fibre and exert more force."

The research team felt that imagined exercise initiated the same motor-programming in the brain as real exercise, and thus improved the neural pathways between the brain and the muscle group involved.

Thus if you are ever unable to complete your exercise practice (Chapter 7 has a guide to *really* keeping yourself fit and healthy), simply imagine, vividly, doing your entire workout. You will derive considerable benefits.

From all the above it can be seen that you are the architect of your own inner space; that the thoughts you have can both increase the actual physical complexity and sophistication of your brain, while at the same time ensuring that the multiple billions of thought patterns you establish are increasingly aligned to help you develop all aspects of your personal being.

As was said in Chapter 1, Your Amazing Synergetic Brain:

"... as you create more and more positive galaxies and universes of thoughts, you will at the same time be forging new physical connections within your brain. You will, literally, be making your super-bio computer more complex, more sophisticated, more powerful, and more successful."

Meta-Positive Thinking, in which you and your individual brain cells are reaching out for new knowledge and learning experiences, in a continually upward spiral of development, is the method by which you create the increasingly sophisticated physical structure and architecture of your brain.

This point was beautifully and amusingly illustrated in research reported at the beginning of this Century of the Brain. Research conducted by a team from University College, London, and the Institute of Neurology, discovered that in London Black Cab taxi drivers, the posterior hippocampus (which governs, among many other things, navigational skills) had increased in size to accommodate the information needed to navigate around the streets of London – "The Knowledge" as it is called in taxi driving parlance. The average cabbie will spend two solid years, studying virtually every day, preparing to be tested on their mastery of the vast number of possible routes, and all their significant buildings and landmarks, between various locations in the vast metropolis of London. Only when they have passed rigorous tests can they be granted a license.

As the *Daily Telegraph* newspaper reported: "It came as no surprise to members of the profession that they enjoy a degree of neurological superiority over the common herd!" The reason? Cabbies have long known that the intense study that they do is more than equivalent to the knowledge required for a first-class Master's degree from a university, and tends, as they report, to enhance and strengthen all their mental skills.

All that you need to do to become the artist, scientist, and architect of your own Cathedrals of Thought, Creativity and Memory, is to apply your own brilliant conglomeration of brain cells to the manufacture of their own increasing sophistication, power and brilliance!

But what, you might still ask, about those still-present old **Big Bad Habits** and the monster **Meta-Negative Thinking Habit**?!

reconsidering the negative-thinking habits

Now that you are well on your way to establishing both **Good New Habits** and the overall **Habit of Meta-Positive Thinking**, what do you think should be done about any existing **Big Bad Habits** and **Meta-Negative Thinking Habits**?

1. Try to forget them?	Yes/No
2. Consciously block them out of your thoughts?	Yes/No
3. Try actively to deconstruct them?	Yes/No
4. Just leave them alone?	Yes/No
5. Ask an expert for advice on how to get rid of them?	Yes/No
6. Ask a brain surgeon to laser them out?	Yes/No
7. Devise a special **Meta-Positive Thinking** affirmation to erase them?	Yes/No

Should we try to forget them?

No! If we do, as you now know, we will remember them even more. And trying to deconstruct them will have exactly the same result.

Should we ask a brain surgeon to laser them out?! Obviously not!

Looked at in the **Meta-Positive** light, these habits are now increasingly becoming history. *Your* history! They are, therefore, your knowledge databanks from life, incorporating many of your experiences and memories. They are a major part of the library of your own life.

In a very real sense the **Big Bad Habit** and the **Meta-Negative Thinking**

Habit, often seen as somehow "bad" or "evil," now begin to play a major part in the development of your ultimate thinking goal: *Wisdom*. Rather than being "enemies of the state," they become friends, adding greater depth and breadth to your life. Rather than discarding them, they should be used to help you increasingly to gain perspective, and to help both yourself and others.

Imagine, for example, that you have just suffered some personal failure. Who do you think would give you most help:

(a) someone who had blocked out all their own bad memories and simply told you to pick yourself up and get on with life, or

(b) someone who explained to you that they had been in a similar situation as you, understood how devastating it was, and who then assured you that you would get through it successfully, as they had done?

Looked at in this **Meta-Positive** light, all the **Big Bad Habits** and the **Meta-Negative Monster** become a major part of your growing wisdom.

meta-positive thinking formula: a summary

The **Meta-Positive Thinking** formula must be:

1. **Personal** ("I" or "we" if it's a group or team)
2. **Real**
3. **Obtainable** (set high obtainable goals!)
4. **Stated in the present** (I/we am/are)
5. **Stated as a process** involving action ("-ing" words: growing/becoming)
6. **Truthful**
7. **Motive –ational.** It must be proactive and give you impetus
8. **Positive and directed to a clear positive vision/image**
9. **Attractive**
10. **Relevant** to your needs
11. **Beneficial** to your overall being

Remember the Olympic Rowing Squad on page 65? A perfect example of Meta-Positive Thinking applied to real and sporting life occurred on the crew's way to the Olympic final. Just two months before the Olympics in Seoul, they were racing in a final of a Regatta on the River Thames against the undefeated Australian Eight.

All bets were on the Australians (except the crew's and mine!) Right from the start, the Australians pulled into a lead of two-thirds of a length, which they maintained until they were only a few hundred meters to go. It is "rowing lore" on this stretch of the Thames that any crew significantly behind at this stage of the race is doomed to defeat.

The Meta-Positive Thinking British squad did not accept this. Their Cox yelled at them that anything was possible, and with a sudden leap, the British boat took nearly a quarter-of-a-length out of the Australians' lead. The Australians, already relaxing into their "assured victory" were taken by surprise, and the British boat maintained its impetus, creeping up inch by inch as they approached the finishing line. It appeared as if it were a dead heat. The crowd waited in suspense for over three minutes before the announcer proclaimed: "In the final of the Grand Challenge Cup between the Australian Olympic Squad and the Olympic Designate Squad from Great Britain, the winners, by a *foot* were Great Britain."

When I spoke to the Cox afterwards, he asked, mischievously and with a smile on his face, "What, Tony, do you think that foot was?" I mused for a moment, and then asked him to tell me.

"A thought!" he beamed.

He was right!

meta-positive thinking workout

1. Check your "self-talk" and discover what **Meta-Habits** (Negative or Positive) you are currently growing.

2. Establish your life goals. (Start to work on bite-size chunks.)

3. Put these goals into **Meta-Positive Thinking** affirmations and repeat them a minimum of five times a day (the more repetitions the merrier!)

4. Realize that as you are doing this you are in the process of improving your Life!

5. Reassess your life, both past and future, in the light of what you now know about how your thinking works, and note down the wisdom gained from any **BBHs** and **MNTHs** you have had.

6. Get into the habit of breaking habits! This will produce a major and paradigm-shifting impact on your life. When you think about it, you will realize that most people are in the habit of *keeping* habits. You will be launching yourself into a **Meta-Positive Habit** of searching out any habit patterns that need improvement, and immediately going to work, using **Meta-Positive Thinking**, to bring about your desired change.

The **MPH**-breaking habit will release you from the tyranny of the accumulated probabilities of your current **BBHs**, and will allow you, with fresh eyes, to know and to adjust yourself towards your life's vision.

brain boosters

Understanding as you now do, the functioning of both your brain cells and your **Meta-Thinking**, you will know precisely how to design and sculpt the **Good New Habit** affirmations you desire. Below is a selection of some that have been found to be particularly useful by myself, and by Olympic athletes.

1. My thinking skills are continuing to improve.
2. I am in the process of becoming fitter and healthier.
3. Every day in every way I am getting better and better.
4. I am increasingly truthful in all my dealings.
5. Honesty is one of my beacons.
6. I am increasingly able to adjust old habits and to generate Positive New Habits.

creative & radiant thinking: using your mind to better your body

Aristotle claimed that the greatest sign of an advanced mind was its ability to think in metaphor (to find striking associations between disparate objects).

introduction

You begin this chapter newly aware of the infinite capacity of your brain cells to make patterns, and the similarly infinite capacity of your brain to use those infinite patterns to generate infinite thoughts.

In this chapter I am going to show you how to apply those two infinities to the wonderful universe of Creative Thinking. This whole chapter can be seen as one giant Brain/Creative Thinking Workout.

The Quick Brain-Check you are about to do will give you a very clear picture of where you are now, to give you a launching pad into your much more Creative future. Along the way you will discover how your own initial results compare with those of other people around the world.

There is also an intriguing Creativity Game for you, which will increasingly open door after door to the realms of your Creative Imagination. As these doors open, I will help you to discover new ways of improving your original performances – these amusing and imagination-stretching exercises will greatly strengthen your Creativity Muscle.

On the basis of the new discoveries you will make about the power of your imagination, I will introduce you to the brilliant **Radiant and Creative Thinking** tool: the Mind Map® – and show you a new way of making your Creative Imagination visible.

Everything you have learned in the chapter will then be combined in new formulas for releasing your poetic soul and for writing poetry, developed by the late English Poet Laureate, Ted Hughes, and myself.

You will finish this chapter with the "body" of your brain, brain cells, thinking, and Creativity in superb shape, and be ready to apply everything you have learned to your **Body Thinking**.

Before launching into an exploration of the explosively interesting area of Creativity with you, I would like you to do a general "Creativity Check-Up" and a standard Creativity game/test. (The answers to the Check-Up are on page 114.)

quick brain-check 9 – creativity

1.	Creativity is an inborn trait. Some people have it, some don't.	True/False?
2.	Creative Thinking cannot be taught.	True/False?
3.	There are fundamental formulas to Creativity. These can be mimicked.	True/False?
4.	Linear note-taking is a good method for triggering creative thought.	True/False?
5.	Circle the term which best describes your creativity level:	

Genius

Superior

Excellent

Very good

Good

Above average

Average

Below average

Poor

Very weak

Absent!

6.   On a scale of zero to 100, where zero = rock-bottom and 100 = genius level, how would you rate yourself as a Creative Thinker?

7.   Give yourself exactly two minutes to write down, as fast as you can, every single use you can think of for a coat-hanger. Finish the exercise, and then continue reading.

Your goal is to find out how many uses for a coat-hanger you thought of per minute. Therefore add up your total number of ideas and divide by two, to give your average output per minute.

Your results will be analyzed shortly.

creativity

Creativity involves the use of the full range of left and right brain mental skills, including:

Words	Rhythm
Logic	Spatial awareness
Numbers	Gestalt (whole picture)
Sequence	Imagination
Linearity	Daydreaming
Analysis	Color
Lists	Dimension

The first group of words – the "left brain skills" – are valued and taught in schools. However, the second group of skills is far less valued and not only are they not taught, they are often actively discouraged in schools.

The young child who is totally open-minded, who adores drawing and painting and who colors all things all colors, who asks incessant questions, and who can imagine that the box in which his birthday present came is an infinite variety of things, including an airplane, a house, a cave, a tank, a boat, and a spaceship, gradually becomes trained to write notes in only one color, to ask very few questions (especially not "stupid" ones – that is, the most interesting ones!), to keep the millions of lusting-for-action muscle fibers still for hours on end, and to become increasingly aware of his incompetences in art, singing, intelligence, and physical sports. In time the child thus graduates into an adult who considers himself uncreative, and who has "progressed" from being able to think of millions of uses for a box to being able to think of hardly any uses for anything!

Let's look at the Creativity Test in Quick Brain-Check 9 again.

the creativity test – global average results

The average number of uses for a coat-hanger per minute scores range from 0 (and this is with some effort!) through 4–5 (which is the global average), to 8 (which is good "brain-stormer" level), 12 (which is exceptional and rare), to 16 – which is Thomas Edison-genius level (see Figure 12).

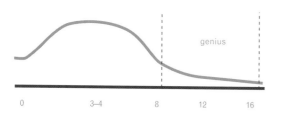

genius

0	3–4	8	12	16

Figure 12: creativity graph

If people are given as long as they want to think up as many uses as they can for a coat-hanger, the average score is 20–30 uses.

There is one further thing that you should know about this test: the results are considered statistically *reliable*. In other words, if you take the test on any given day, and then years later take it again, your results will be similar. Like IQ-scores, your height and the color of your eyes, your creativity score is thought to be a permanent feature of your personality profile. The statistical findings of reliability have been based upon decades-worth of research and thousands of psychological creativity studies.

Recalling all that you have learned so far in *Head Strong*, doesn't something here strike you as a little odd?!

Imagine that you are a salesperson, who is trying to convince a customer to "buy brains."

You go through all your sales patter – you tell them that you have the most amazing product in the universe. You explain that each brain is a super bio-computer and each has a million million super bio-computer microchips. You point out that the number of patterns of intelligence your company's brains can make is the number one followed by ten-and-a-half million kilometers of zeros.

You go on to mention that these particular brains can remember virtually anything as long as they use special memory techniques, showing off their ability to link any object with any other object. You throw in that your superb product can think, speak multiple languages, solve mathematical problems, see, hear, smell, taste, touch, and operate its associated body magnificently.

Finally you reach the climax of your presentation, and inform the customer that this amazing product can think of four or five uses for a coat-hanger in a minute, and about 25 in a lifetime! Sale closed?!

Juxtaposing this information about the brain puts in stark relief the fact that there is, indeed, something seriously wrong. Something wrong both with the way we have been trained to use our brains, *and* the above creativity test as a true measure of our creative potential.

further examination of the creativity test

Go back to your original uses for your coat-hanger and circle the one you think is your most creative idea. When you have chosen it, jot down the criteria that made you choose it. You chose it because it was the most ... what?

Now check the following list of words and mark the ones you think best define an idea that is creative:

(a) Normal

(b) Original

(c) Practical

(d) Removed from the norm

(e) Bland

(f) Exciting

The obvious answers are that creative ideas need to be *original* and *removed from the norm*, and, as such, they are usually *exciting*.

If you come up with the idea that you could use a coat-hanger to hang coats on, no one is going to beat a path to your door! However, if you thought of using it to form sculptures, or to make a musical instrument, people will be far more interested not only in your ideas, but in you too.

If you think about it, the great geniuses, by definition, had to be "removed from the norm." If Stravinsky had written music like all those before him, we would never have heard of him. Similarly if Picasso had painted like his predecessors, instead of in his astoundingly original style, we also would never have known of him.

The creative genius lives at the upper end of the creativity curve. This explains why the general population will often consider them mad, because their ideas are so removed from the norm that it is difficult for someone not trained in Creative Thinking to understand the new associations that the genius is making!

From now on you will have a much deeper understanding of the nature of the thoughts of the genius. You are well on your way to becoming one yourself.

looking again at the creativity test

Tests of the sort you have just taken have been given to tens of thousands of people over the last few decades. The psychologists who administer them have confirmed that they are reliable – if you take a similar test five, ten, fifteen years from now, you will tend to score roughly the same as you did a couple of pages ago.

But is this really so? Or has your brain-selling attempt opened the way to other conclusions?

Indeed it has.

Let's look again at the question – "Think of every possible use you can for a coat-hanger."

The more rigidly taught mind will assume that "uses" refer to the standard, ordinary, sensible applications for a coat-hanger. That same rigidly taught mind will also assume that the coat-hanger is of a standard size and is made of the standard material. Standard, standard, standard = normal, normal, normal thinking. And norm-al thinking is average. Indeed, the very word "normal" was born from the statistical "norm."

What is the Creativity Test trying to measure? Thoughts that are *away* from the norm.

The Mentally Literate®, and therefore more flexibly taught brain, will see far more opportunities for creative interpretations of the question, and therefore will generate both *more* ideas and ideas of higher *quality*. The Mentally Literate® and creative mind will expand the meaning of the word "uses" to include the phrase "connections with." It will also realize immediately that the coat-hanger could be of any size, made of any material, and be transformed into any shape.

The creative genius will therefore break all the ordinary boundaries, and will include in the list of uses, many "far out" (away from the norm!) applications, such as "melting a five-ton metal coat-hanger and pouring it into a giant mold to make the hull of a boat."

As you can see, the Mentally Literate® creative individual is naturally tapping in to the brain's basic physical capacity to make *one-followed-by-ten-and-a-half-million-kilometers-of-zeros*-worth of associations.

A mere 2,000 or so uses for *any* standard object, to such a mind, is only the start!

quick brain-check 10 – creativity game

To test for yourself that this concept is true – that your own and anyone else's creative thinking can be taught and improved – try the following new Creativity Test, using your new knowledge of how your Creative Mind works.

Listed below are 40 randomly generated words. Your task (or you and your friends – this is a good game to play with others) is to find uses/associations between a coat-hanger and each of the listed words.

Some of these may seem difficult at first, but if you persevere and look for wider and wilder interpretations, you *will* find an association.

At the end of the list you will find examples thought up by my students, friends and myself. If you come up with ideas that are more "far out" than ours, give yourself some extra congratulations!

Enjoy the journey into your newly Creative Imagination!

1. Golf ball
2. Snow
3. Lock
4. Muscle
5. Mussel
6. Music
7. Circus
8. Back
9. Plant
10. Flag

11. Shoe

12. Potato

13. Pipe

14. Pen

15. Solar System

16. Knife

17. Money

18. Clock

19. Ice

20. Animal

21. Soup bowl

22. Light bulb

23. Salt

24. Hair

25. Communication

26. Drinking straw

27. Tree

28. Fish

29. Bull

30. Juggling

31. Chocolates

32. Swan

33. Balloon

34. Giant

35. Microbe

36. Sheep

37. Moon

38. Jaw

39. Magnifying glass

40. Ship

possible associations/uses for "the list of 40"

1. **Golf ball** The coat-hanger could be used to retrieve golf balls from unfriendly ponds or ditches. A large coat-hanger could be molded into an extra golf club in cases of emergency.

2. **Snow** By lashing leather around it, you could transform a coat-hanger into a snow shoe. By lashing some more solid object into its triangular "window" you could fashion a primitive ski or sled.

3. **Lock** A coat-hanger could make a perfect key or lock-opener (indeed, creative crooks often use them as tools for breaking into vehicles!)

4. **Muscle** A coat-hanger of a thick resilient material such as silicon or reinforced rubber could be used as an isometric muscle-training device.

5. **Mussel** A coat-hanger could make a perfect tool for both opening the shell of the mussel and for scooping out the meat within.

6. **Music** The coat-hanger is a ready-made triangle!

7. **Circus** A coat-hanger could be used as the hoop through which animals jump. The size of the coat-hanger would depend upon the size of the animal...

8. **Back** Scratcher!

9. **Plant** A coat-hanger would make an idea plant trainer.

10. **Flag** A coat-hanger could act as a flagpole. It could also be used to keep the furled flag in place.

11. **Shoe** An ideal shoe horn!

12. **Potato** A perfect spit for holding your baking potato over the blazing flames.

13. **Pipe** Cleaner!

14. **Pen** Use your coat-hanger to scratch messages on rock; to write messages in clay; or you could file the end off at an angle, dip it in ink and use it as a standard pen.

15. **Solar System** Use your coat-hanger to hang models of the sun and the nine planets from a schoolroom ceiling, in order to teach the children about the local neighborhood of our universe.

16. **Knife** A coat-hanger can easily be transformed into a cutting device.

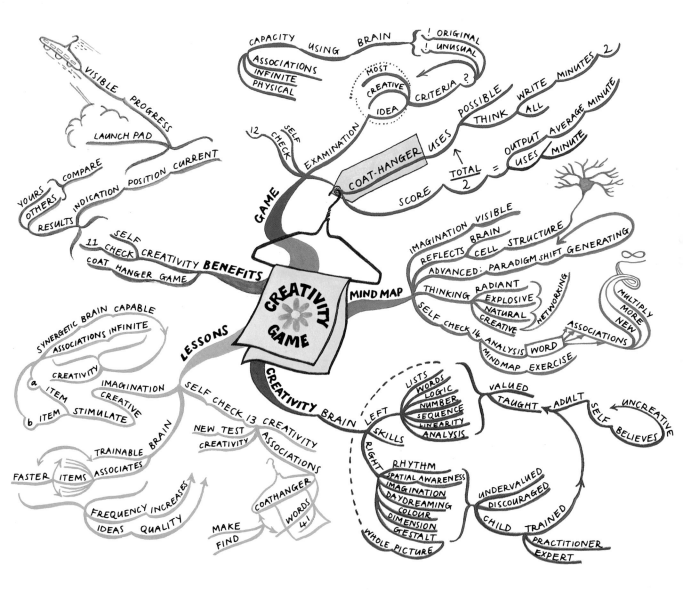

Mind Map® 11

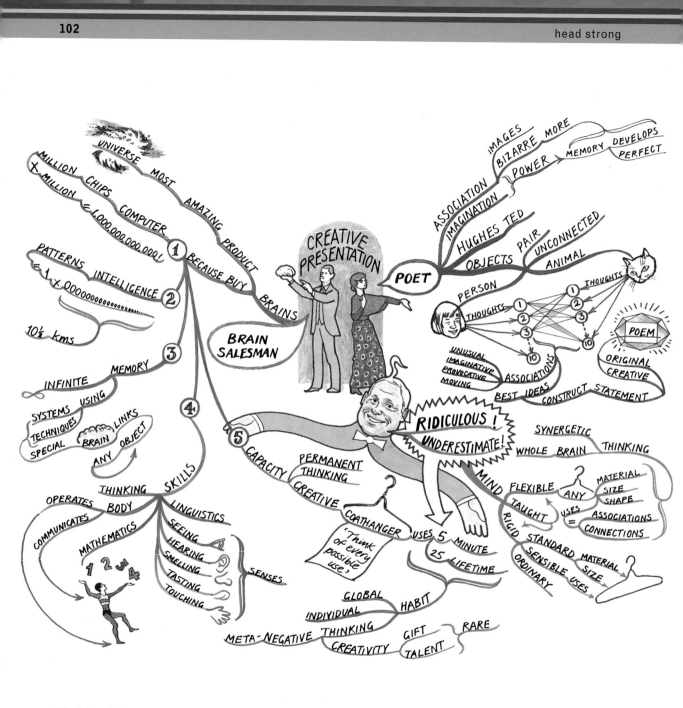

Mind Map® 12

17. **Money** Use a coat-hanger to barter with if someone desperately needs one, or use a gold coat-hanger to trade for anything you want!

18. **Clock** By sticking a coat-hanger upright in the ground, you can use it as a sun dial, the casting of its shadow accurately telling you the time.

19. **Ice** A super-cooled coat-hanger could be used to make ice.

20. **Animal** A coat-hanger could be an animal's toy, or could be used to release a trapped animal.

21. **Soup bowl** A big coat-hanger made of metal could be pounded flat and then easily sculpted into a soup bowl.

22. **Light bulb** A coat-hanger could be used as the filament in a bulb.

23. **Salt** A coat-hanger is an ideal instrument for unclogging the salt shaker or for separating the particles in salt that has become clumped.

24. **Hair** The point of the coat-hanger could be used as a primitive and simple comb. The whole coat-hanger could also be used as a foundation piece for a punk-rocker's hair-do!

25. **Communication** An ideal instrument for tapping out the Morse code.

26. **Drinking straw** A thick coat-hanger could be tunneled out, and would immediately be useful as a straw.

27. **Tree** Coat-hangers are made for clothes trees!

28. **Fish** Hook.

29. **Bull** Nose-ring or matador's weapon.

30. **Juggling** If jugglers can juggle with balls, flaming clubs, guns, chickens and chain-saws, why not coat-hangers?!

31. **Chocolates** Wonderful for spearing chocolates from the box. Decorative candy coat-hangers covered in chocolate are a delight!

32. **Swan** A coat-hanger would be an ideal object for helping a novice art student trace the first basic shapes of this elegant bird.

33. **Balloon** Popping! Tying the nozzle of. Hanging and displaying.

34. **Giant** Could use it as a knitting needle, an ordinary needle or a pin.

35. **Microbe** At the microscopic level, the surface of any coat-hanger will be riddled with caves – perfect homes for microbes.

36. **Sheep** On which to hang its transformed fleece!

37. **Moon** A gigantic coat-hanger could be transformed into a space ship.

38. **Jaw** A metal coat-hanger could be used to "wire up" a broken jaw.

39. **Magnifying glass** A glass coat-hanger (and quite a few exist) has curvatures that can bend light into magnified images.

40. **Ship** Anchor. Rudder. Sail clip. All-purpose tool. (You should never sail without one!)

A number of lessons can be learned from this exercise:

1. That the way to stimulate your Creative Imagination is *not* to spend time looking for a possible use or association. This is just a case of searching in an infinite darkness. The correct way is to *give* your brain any other item. With the two in place your brain will automatically go into **"Synergetic Association Mode,"** and will, inevitably, find a link of some sort.

2. That if you apply this second, Correct Formula, your brain can link *anything with anything* – this exercise has just domonstrated your brain's infinite capacity to create associations and to generate Creative Thought.

   It is interesting to note here the words and advice of Leonardo da Vinci, the man most often regarded the greatest creative genius of all time. Da Vinci said that one of the principles by which he operated, and by which he generated his own creative thinking, was the observation that:
   "Everything in some way connects to everything else."

   Not surprisingly da Vinci was using the **Synergetic Brain Principle,** and giving his ten-and-a-half-million-kilometers-of-thoughts-worth of pattern-making possibilities a lot about which to think!

3. We also learn from this exercise that when you *do* give your brain items to link, it will associate them together with accelerating speed. Your brain *can* be trained to improve!

4. In addition you will have observed that the more you use this "paired

association" technique for Creative Thinking, the more wild and far out your ideas will become. And in the context of Creativity, what do "wild and far out" mean? Good *quality* Creativity!

5. A further realization from this last point is that Creative Thinking leads to humor and the probability of more humor! Humor is one of the hallmarks of the Creative Mind – develop your wit and you will be improving the power of your Creative Intelligence.

6. Our last realization comes from your earlier attempts to sell brains: the absurd final pitch that the customer should buy a brain because "this amazing product can think of four or five uses for a coat-hanger in a minute, and 25 in a life time!" How can this Creativity Test possibly be statistically fixed and "reliable" when you have just demonstrated that you could easily write down 20 or 30 uses in a minute, and can continue at that pace for the rest of your life!

    The disturbing truth, however, is that the tests *have* been reliable. They have been reliably measuring the *phenomenal power of a* **Meta-Negative Thinking Habit**; a habit that has built up not only in most individual brains, but in the global brain as well – the habit of thinking that "I am not creative," and that "creativity is a rare talent gifted to only one in 10 million."

    It is a habit so strong that it has held billions of individuals, for hundreds of years, in the prison of assuming that they could only think of a very few uses for anything, when, in fact, they could think up an infinite number of uses if only they had allowed themselves; in the prison of thinking, there are only a few solutions to an infinite number of problems, when the truth is that *there are an infinite number of solutions to a relatively small number of problems*.

    This new knowledge gives us a much brighter picture of our future. Armed with it there is another exercise you can do to demonstrate your brain's infinite thinking capability, while simultaneously self-developing the ultimate Creative Thinking tool.

the creative Mind Map® – the ultimate creative thinking tool

Traditional methods of brain-storming have required one individual to stand at a board and list all the ideas that are given by the group.

From what you know about the brain's **synergetic** thinking, about its infinitely associative physical pathways, and about its creative capacity to form links and associations in all directions, you will realize that linear note-taking and list-making is the *worst* way you can choose to encourage your brain's creativity! Lines and lists put your brain behind prison-bars that methodically disconnect and cut off each thought from every other thought. It is like taking a pair of scissors and snipping the connections between your brain cells.

What your brain needs is a Creative Thinking tool that reflects its natural way of functioning – which allows it to use all its images and associations in the explosive and networking way to which it was born, which internally it always uses, and to which you need to allow it to become *re*-accustomed.

This thinking tool is called a Mind Map®, and it is based on integrating everything you have so far learned in *Head Strong*.

Below you will find a basic Mind Map®. A Mind Map® contains a basic image or word at its center. This immediately triggers the power of your Creative imagination. From this image radiate main branches of thought associated with the central image. These branches are curved because your brain prefers organic structures to rigid ones, and they are large because the size represents the importance of the ideas.

You can see from this image that your brain is *not* a linear-thinking device. Your brain is a **Radiant Thinking**® organ. The associations and radiations from the brain's central thinking images eerily reflect, in structure, your brain cells (see Figure 5, page 32). The Mind Map®, in its turn, reflects this too.

Figure 13: basic Mind Map®

quick brain-check 11 – creative Mind Map® exercise

The Mind Map® opposite has, as its central image, the human being. Copy the image yourself onto a large piece of paper. On each of the main branches print clearly the first five words that come into your mind when you think of the concept "Human Being." You are recommended to print the words because printed words give a more immediate feedback to your brain, and allow the Creative process to happen more rapidly.

When you have completed this, go to the branch which has a further five "twigs" added, and write down the first five thoughts that come into your mind when you associate the key thought from which your five new words will spray. As you do this exercise, notice just how your brain is functioning.

analysis of quick brain-check 11

What you have just demonstrated with this Creative Mind Map® exercise is that, once again, your Creative Thinking ability is potentially infinite. Every time you put down any word on a Mind Map®, it will automatically give rise to new associations. Those new associations will give rise to their own associations, which will multiply to give even more associations, and the positive spiral continues on, cascading to infinity.

And even that is not where it ends! If you look at your developing Mind Map® again, you will realize that you could go on infinitely in any one of the 360 degrees that your Mind Map® allows you to explore. Even more than that, if you had a spherical Mind Map® image in the center, you could continue associating infinitely off an infinite number of radials!

Your brain is a Creative Thinking machine, capable of an *infinity of infinities* of creative thoughts.

This ties neatly back into Professor Anokhin's calculations of the number of physical patterns of thought, which the Professor claimed as infinite. You have just confirmed, twice (first in the Creativity Game and now in the Creative Mind Map® Exercise), that this indeed is the case.

advanced creative Mind Mapping® – generating the paradigm shift

As you explore any subject with a Creative Mind Map® you will see that words which initially did not seem particularly significant will occasionally pop up on the outer limits of one branch, and then another, and then another.

If such a word or concept appears twice, simply underline it in each instance, to make it stand out from the background. Should that same word pop up a third time, it is probably worth putting a small box around it, as it is obviously of growing importance, and certainly deserves more emphasis than words that appear only once.

In certain instances you will find a word that appears on four or more branches, or even on all the branches of your developing Creative Mind Map®. If this happens, put the box into three dimensions.

At this stage you can use your cortical skills of dimension and Gestalt (your brain's ability to see the "whole picture") to help bring about a major shift and advance in your thinking on the subject. First you dimensionalize the boxes around the key concept. Next you link the boxes to form a giant box; and then you dimensionalize that box.

In what does your original Mind Map® now nestle? A new *framework*. In other words, your mind has realized that the original network of thought is actually contained within a larger framework, and that a word/concept you originally thought was minor is, in fact, so major that it pervades your subject, and may well warrant being made the new center for your next Creative Mind Map® on the topic.

This is called a **Paradigm Shift** in thinking, and it is the goal of all great thinkers. Beethoven paradigm-shifted our appreciation of emotion and music;

Cézanne paradigm-shifted the perception of all artists after him; Magellan paradigm-shifted the flat earth to a global planet; Copernicus paradigm-shifted the universe inside out; Einstein paradigm-shifted our perceptions of the nature of that universe.

The **Creative Thinking** Mind Map® is a thinking tool designed to accelerate the appearance of Paradigm Shifts, and thus to enhance the global output of Creative Thought. Use it to enhance your own Creativity, and as a constant reminder of just how infinite your Creative Thinking capabilities are.

One final example of a **Creative Thinking Paradigm Shift** Mind Map® comes from my own work on Memory. Figure 14 is a very simplified version of a Mind Map® that was, in fact, gigantic, and which took me years to build and grow. The Mind Map® is a summary of my own research and explorations into the tantalizing world of Memory.

The more I explored, the more I realized that every single area of Memory – whether it be how we remember during learning, how we remember after learning, why we forget, what historical memory

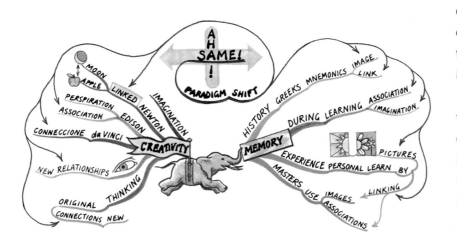

Figure 14: memory Mind Map®

techniques were, or what approaches the great memorizers use – there were always two words that kept on recurring.

I linked these and framed them on my giant Mind Map®. I then came to the paradigm-shifting realization that, underlying everything one could learn about memory were two massive foundation principles: if you wish to improve your memory, you have to train your *Imagination*, and you have to enhance your ability to *Associate*. There was more to come!

I had been simultaneously studying Creativity, building up a similar giant Mind Map®. As you now already know from this chapter, what are the two main tools of Creativity? *Imagination* and *Association*!

My Mind Maps®, which themselves were developed as thinking tools based on Association and Imagination, had led me to two paradigm shifts. These two then led me to a **Meta-Paradigm Shift**: that Creativity and Memory are *virtually identical* mental processes, used for different ends. The **Meta-Paradigm Shift** demonstrated that the Mind Map® is at first a *divergent* thinking tool, which, by its very structure, then encourages *convergent* thinking at the next level. This creates sparks of divergent thinking, and so on and on...

From this came the pleasing (and time-saving!) realization that:

When you train your Creativity, you automatically train your Memory
When you train your Memory, you automatically train your Creative Thinking skills!

While you have been developing your **Creative Thinking** skills in this chapter, you have, *with no extra effort*, been enhancing the power of your Memory. You are already involved in a **synergetically** positive spiral that will continue to improve both your **Creative Thinking** and your Memory for the rest of your life.

The Creative Mind Maps® found throughout this book, summarizing important areas in *Head Strong*, should be even more meaningful and helpful to you now!

Let's put what you have learned to a practical **Creative Thinking** use – the writing of poetry.

poetry – the use of creative Mind Maps®

Ted Hughes, the great English Poet Laureate of the 20th century, was a passionate believer in creating what he called "Warriors of the Mind." He developed a wonderful technique for developing creative and metaphorical thinking, in which he used memory systems and Mind Maps®. You can duplicate the process.

First he would teach his students simple memory systems, to prove to them that by using the powers of *Association* and *Imagination*, their memories could develop to a level of perfect performance. Hughes used to emphasize that the more bizarre (removed from the norm!) their images were, the better their memories would be.

Having broken through the mental blocks in their imaginations, and encouraged those imaginations to run wild, Hughes took them through an exercise very similar to that which you did when linking the concept "coat-hanger" to the 40 new objects.

He would give his students a pair of apparently completely disconnected objects and would ask them to do the Mind Map® exercise, identical to the one you did on "Human Being," for each of the objects.

When the students had associated 10 words around each concept, Ted Hughes would then instruct them to take one word from one concept and find associations with the 10 words from the other. They then moved to the second word from the first concept and found associations for it with the 10 words from the other, and so on until they had associated all 10 with all 10. Many of the associations were extremely unusual, highly imaginative, very provocative, and often quite moving.

The students' next task was to select the best ideas from all their thoughts, and from them to construct a creative and original statement, and ideally a poem.

One of Hughes' favorite exercises was to juxtapose "one," a person, and "one," an animal. The exercise was the same: radiate 10 thoughts on the first, 10 thoughts on the second, and then find the most enticing associations.

For your own amusement I have given a list of "opposites" for you to play with in your creative imagination. You can simply read them, finding at least two associations between each as you go along, or do the poetry writing Mind Map® exercise on each, and write your own creative pieces from them.

- Speed – Calm
- Pawn – Wealth
- Match – Mate
- Star – Trend
- Go – Wall

- Bored – Board
- Queen – King
- Humans – Computers
- Bull – Email
- Sun – Lake

I did Ted Hughes' Mind Map® approach to poetry on the theme of *Head Strong: Body and Mind*. I took the main key words, and played with them, arranging them so that each word had multiple meanings/associations (see Figure 15). I hope you enjoy playing with them as much as I did!

The result is the poem opposite, which also acts as a mini-summary of the purpose of this book!

creativity workout

This chapter itself has been a Creativity Workout for you! To continue growing the power of your Creativity Muscle, try the following:

1. Keep using the full range of your mental skills.
2. Keep stretching your thinking beyond the norm.
3. Play variations on the Creativity Game regularly – take any object and associate it with as many other things as you possibly can, in the same way as you did with the coat-hanger.
4. Develop a sense of humor!
5. Use Mind Maps® for any Creative Thinking you ever do. Then, think creatively about other uses for Mind Maps®!
6. Review the Mind Maps® in *Head Strong*, copying as many ideas from them as you can to help you develop your own creativity in Mind Map® making.
7. Actively search for Paradigm Shifts in your thinking. Have courage and actively look for opportunities to change your perspectives on your habitual beliefs.
8. Make writing poetry part of the new you.

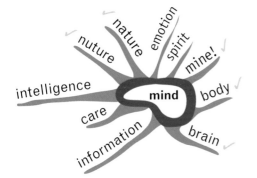

Figure 15: body and mind Mind Maps®

My Body;
My Mind
Brain
Food: Food
            O_2
            Info
            Love
Me.

Nurture nature

Mind body
Mind mine

Makes
Good
Sense

Mine body
Mine mind

Gold

Mine!
Mine!!
Mine!!!

brain boosters

1. I am by design a Creative Thinker.
2. My ability to make new associations is infinite.
3. I increasingly use this ability to improve my memory and to enhance my Creativity.
4. I am increasingly using the power of Imagination and Association to develop my sense of humor.
5. My thinking is by nature Radiant. I use this to generate radiance and to visualize, organize, and generate thoughts.
6. I am a natural poet. I allow my new knowledge of my brain and thinking to help release the infinite creative thoughts waiting for expression.

answers to quick brain-check 9

1. False
2. False
3. True
4. False
5. Interestingly, in this test "average" people rate themselves as "below average."
6. Similarly to the previous question, most people rate themselves as "below average."

In Part III, I will introduce you to the miraculous piece of equipment that is your body, and the intimate and synergetic relationship that is possible between it and your brain. I will introduced you to the revolutionary Olympian **Success Training Formula – TEFCAS –** and you will be given some health, training and conditioning advice, designed to maximize your **Brain** and **Body Thinking**.

healthy body, healthy mind

the revolutionary success formula – tefcas
your body: how to develop and use it well
brain and body food
stress-busting, healing and more…

helpful and positive "*How fascinating*!" This leaves our senses far more open to the experience, and allows us to get the full and valuable **Feedback** from what was once called a "failure," and which we now realize is simply another **Event**.

Many people report that, some time after a major Big Black Hole, they realize that it was this **Event** that gave them major new insights and strengths. Has it been the same with you?

After having **Checked** the **Feedback** from our Big Black Hole, what are we obliged to do next? **Adjust** toward our positive goal of **Success** and try again. As you continue applying your **TEFCAS Success Formula**, you will inevitably rise and fall as you progress. If, however, you persist, you will, also inevitably, suddenly experience the opposite of the Big Black Hole: the giant Star of Success.

Surprisingly, even **Success** holds its own dangers. Some love this triumph so much that they are afraid to try again, for fear that they will never return to such giddy heights. Some set their goals too low and too much in the short term, and suddenly, to their despair, find that they have nowhere left to go.

One of the best examples of this was in a recent Olympic semi-final, in which one of the runners in the 400 meters had made it to the final. He was interviewed by international television after the race, and exclaimed ecstatically to the interviewer, "This is amazing! It's fantastic! I've always wanted to be in the Olympic Final! It's my dream come true!" And off he happily jogged.

What do you think happened to him in the final? Last! Why? Because his brain and body had already done what he had instructed them to – get him to the Olympic final. The goal was already reached. Once he was in the final it didn't matter what he did – he could have *walked* – because he was *there*. In the final, you could see that all his motivation had gone.

What does the **TEFCAS Brain Success Formula** say you *should* do after a major **Success**? Celebrate, obviously, and then, as you did with every other **Trial**, say "How fascinating!" **Check** that **Success**, gather all the valuable information from it that you can, **Adjust** toward your far-reaching goals, and **Try** again.

the learning plateau

At some stage in your **TEFCAS** career, you will hit a patch of apparent flatness. You will Try and Try and Try and Try, and for some reason your performance will remain the same. This can go on for weeks, months, and sometimes even years. It happens regularly in athletics and sports, and in academic situations where people become accustomed to getting "Cs" in languages, "As" in science, and "Ds" in history, for example.

Continuous trying and continued non-improvement can lead to a feeling of hopelessness and despair. A mini Black Hole begins to form, and **Meta-Negative** thoughts such as "I've reached my peak," "What's the point of going on?" "I'll never really be any good at this," begin to creep into the thinking process.

Worry not!

What you are experiencing at this stage is what is commonly called a Learning Plateau. Like the Big Black Hole and the Star of Success, the Learning Plateau is a natural and expected part of your learning progress. During the time when you are experiencing a Learning Plateau, your brain (contrary to expectations), will *not* be inactive. It will be doing a number of possible things: integrating everything it has learned so far; consolidating good knowledge and practice;

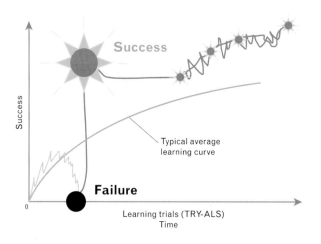

Figure 20: graph showing the inevitability of continuing Success if you continue to apply the TEFCAS Formula

sorting and organizing masses of data acquired over your entire learning experience; and, hopefully and importantly, getting a little bit of needed Rest and Recuperation!

Faults that people make at this Mini Black Hole is that they look into the future, and inaccurately predict an eternal monotony.

They are looking in the wrong direction!

What they need to do is look *back* over from whence they have come. If they do they will notice something very unusual about the learning curve: for the first time in its history it has become *stable*.

What this means, very significantly, is that for many many **Trials** you have not dipped *below* this plateau level. You have established a *new norm* – a new fundamental level. This new base and foundation provides you with tremendous stability and allows you to use it as the new springboard and launching pad for your next foray into further **Success** (see Figure 20).

When you reach the Mini Black Hole, what does **TEFCAS** say you should give your brain? **Feedback**! At this stage you can intensify your learning and feedback systems, and can do a number of things to help this, and to break out into further successes.

You can:

1. Join a relevant club.
2. Take an advanced course.
3. Subscribe to the subject magazines.
4. Give your friends as much information as you can and ask them for feedback.
5. Read further books on the subject.
6. Where appropriate video yourself so that you can analyze your performance.
7. Ask around your circle of friends, relatives and colleagues to see if they know any useful expert contacts for you, and persuade them to introduce you. People are almost always pleased and honored to be approached by someone who is fascinated in their own field of knowledge and who would like help and advice.

Having acquired all this wonderful new feedback, you apply **TEFCAS** again. You assimilate all your new **Feedback, Adjust** your efforts to your determined goal of **Success**, and **Try** again.

When you continue to apply the **Success Formula** and persist in your **Trying**, you will inevitably create more and more **Successes**. If you look at the graph in Figure 20, it will probably remind you of a number of traditional sayings about **Success** that have been handed down through the ages:

Success breeds Success.

This does not mean that when you are successful you simply lie back and say "Fine, I've been successful, so I'll just hang around and let it breed!" It means that once you have been successful, if you *continue* to put more effort into it, **Success** will become increasingly easy and natural.

Nothing succeeds like Success.

As you are increasingly realizing, nothing *does* succeed like **Success**. Remember, *Repetition increases the probability of Repetition*. Your brain is a **Success mechanism!**

If at first you don't succeed try, try and try again

It is important to remember that the saying is *not:* "If at first you don't succeed … try again!" The subtle distinction between "try" and "try, try, try" is one that the wise elders who passed these sayings down were deeply aware was the difference between failure and success. The simple "try" is missing one of the important ingredients of **Meta-Positive Thinking** – it contains within it no admonition toward the ongoing repetition; no persuasion to continue the loop; no determination. It is a one-off.

"Try, try and try" means that you *Try* as a matter of course, and that you always continue to *Try*...

Don't judge those who try and fail
Judge those who fail to try.

Thomas Henry Huxley

These success sayings, and the whole **TEFCAS** model, assume throughout the presence of a mental quality that is so important that it, like the **Success Principle**, has risen to the status of another Brain Principle: **PERSISTENCE**.

brain principle number 5 – persistence

If you never give up, you are a winner.

John Akhwari, last in the 1968 Mexico City Olympic marathon, after battling through serious injury and exhaustion to finish the race

Persistence has often been seen not as a characteristic of intelligence, but as a characteristic of the *opposite* of intelligence. Those who display persistence are often labelled "stubborn," "inflexible," and any one of the various "headeds": "pig...," "bull...," "thick...," "hard...!"

Not only is this *not* the case, the very opposite is true...

Persistence is in fact the *engine* of learning and intelligence. It is the engine of all creative effort, and of all genius. Most importantly, it is the **Try** in **TEFCAS**.

The importance of **Persistence** was summed up best by the most productive creative mind of the last 300 years, Thomas Edison, who holds the record for the largest number of individual patents registered. As well as being famous for his invention of the light bulb (among many other things), Edison is equally renowned for his famous quotation about genius:

Genius is 1 percent inspiration; 99 percent perspiration.

Perspiration = Persistence!

Perhaps one of the greatest ever examples of **Persistence**, turned into a training discipline and ritual that produced one of the greatest body and mind performances in history, is the story of Sir Steve Redgrave, CBE and his five Olympic gold medals. As you read, consider all the principles from *Head Strong* that Steve successfully applied.

persistence and "the greatest olympian of them all"

In the Sydney Olympics in 2000 one athlete stood out from all the other outstanding athletes: Steve Redgrave. Redgrave stood out not only from these athletes, but from the great Olympians of all time.

Why?

Because he had, using the power of his own vision and his persistent commitment to the Ritual of Training, accomplished "the impossible."

As a young boy, Redgrave had not been considered particularly bright, and was given few chances to "make a mark" in the world. However, he was able to "discover" rowing.

At the top level, rowing is considered to be one of the toughest of all sports, because of the commitment to the training ritual it requires, and because of the incredible levels of fitness needed. Unlike many sports, rowing requires you to be fit in three ways: in stamina, flexibility and strength. To train and maintain these three fitnesses requires an incredible amount of dedication.

The training, for example, for one standard day (and remember this has to be done 360 days every year!) would include a 5:00 a.m. wake-up call, followed by two hours of rowing training on the river. After breakfast and a brief relaxation period, one or two hours would be spent reviewing and planning. Another training session, in the gym or on rowing machines, would be followed by lunch and another rest and relaxation period. In the afternoon it would be out on the water again for another two to three hour session of long-distance rowing.

By the age of 22 Redgrave had already put in four such years of commitment to this daily ritual, and in Los Angeles he won his first Olympic Gold.

Four years later, in the 1988 Olympic Games in Seoul, Korea, he had put in another four years of dedicated training, and won his second Gold medal.

By 1992 and the Olympic games in Barcelona, Steve Redgrave had put in another four years of training (that's 12 non-stop years!), and won his third Olympic Gold.

Are you getting exhausted just by the thought of what he had done?!

By 1996 Redgrave had put in another four years of commitment (that's 16 years on the trot!), and won his fourth Olympic Gold.

By this stage many people were already considering Steve Redgrave to be the greatest Olympic athlete ever, for no one had won four consecutive Olympic golds in an endurance sport before. This was still not enough for him.

After some contemplation, he decided to train at the same level of intensity for another four years (that's 20 years in total!!) and to go for his fifth medal at the Sydney Olympics. Then the going got even tougher. A year before the Olympics Redgrave, who had already reached the age of 37 (an age considered by most to be well "over the hill" in terms of top-level rowing), was diagnosed with severe diabetes, and had to add to his training regime insulin injections six times a day.

Steve took on this added responsibility and load, incorporated it into his daily ritual, went to the Sydney Olympics, and won his fifth Olympic Gold!

What is often overlooked in that 20 years of extraordinary commitment to a vision of excellence and to a training ritual of unparalleled intensity, is that throughout that time, at local regattas, national championships, regional championships, World Championships, and Olympic events, in all the races he competed in, including qualifiers, quarter-finals, semi-finals and finals, Steve Redgrave was almost never defeated! What's more, in each of his Olympics, he competed in different boats, with different crews – it was Steve who was the common **Success Factor**!

In rowing, there is a motto which most of the great rowers live by: "Miles Makes Champions." This means that it is the **Persistence** of regular practice both on and off the water which is the "secret formula" that leads to the Olympic Gold.

Steve Redgrave is the ultimate example of how **Persistence** and a valid Life Vision can transform a boy given little hope of success into the "greatest Olympian of all time," and into a person who stands as a shining example of the principles of *Head Strong*. In recognition of his incredible mental and physical brilliance and stamina, Redgrave has been showered with many honors and awards, including a Knighthood.

success formula workout

You will now realize that the **Success Formula TEFCAS**, as well as being a perfect reflection of the Scientific Method of study *and* the child's method for learning, is also a perfect reflection of two other things:

1. The brain cell and the way it associates, imagines and learns.
2. **Meta-Positive Thinking**.

All the previous workouts in *Head Strong* are therefore ones you should continue to do using the **Success Formula**.

From this moment on, emphasize in all your learning and actions the fact that you are leaving your fear of failure behind, that you are applying the **Brain Principle of Persistence** to everything you do, and that you are **learning with every Trial**.

Your Success Formula Workout for this chapter is to apply everything you have learned in it to the next three chapters!

Far better is to dare mighty things, to win glorious triumphs even though checkered by failure, than to rank with those poor spirits who neither enjoy nor suffer much because they live in the gray twilight that knows neither victory nor defeat.

Theodore Roosevelt, 26th President of the United States

brain boosters

1. I am a being based on **Trial** and **Success**.
2. I encourage **Success** to breed from my **Success**.
3. When the name of the game is **Persistence**, **Persistence** is my name!
4. When I am learning, I constantly **Check** the **Events** of that learning.
5. I treasure the **Feedback** my senses give me, and strive to keep them healthy, attuned and alert.
6. My goals are increasingly directed toward positive outcomes.
7. I am designed for **Success**!

chapter seven

your body – how to develop and use it well

Good health is the bedrock on which social progress is built. A nation of healthy people can do things that make life worthwhile, and as the level of health increases, so does the potential for happiness.

Marc Lalonde, former Canadian Minister of National Health and Welfare

Before I consider heart surgery, I always feel the patient's thigh. If the thigh is firm, I know the surgeon is going to find a strong heart to work on when he gets inside. But if the thigh is flabby, the heart's going to be the same.

Dr. Paul Dudley White, Cardiologist to President Eisenhower

introduction

Have you ever wondered, or perhaps even scoffed at, the extraordinary claims made by health-and-fitness books and magazines? On the psychological front, they promise you that if you become healthy you will:

- Experience giant leaps in self-confidence, self-respect and self-empowerment
- Attract more people to you
- Improve general relationships
- Gain respect from family, friends, colleagues and people at large
- Enrich your sex life
- Increase your probability of a better job
- Reduce mental stress and tension

On the physical front, they once again promise that a good fitness and health routine will:

- Give you stronger muscles
- Produce firmer and more resilient bones
- Encourage the development of more and more healthy blood vessels
- Improve the quality of your lungs
- Lower your risk of diseases such as diabetes, osteoporosis, arthritis and cancer
- Lessen your chance of physical injury
- Strengthen and make more resilient your heart

How *can* they promise this apparent Utopia?
Because, extraordinarily, *it is true*!

In the last few decades of the 20th century, and in the first two years of the 21st, gigantic strides have been made in discovering and understanding both how our bodies function, and how to train them, internally and externally, for maximum health. In this chapter I am going to introduce you to a complete awareness of your body, how to look after it and how to use it well.

I am going to introduce you to the four pillars of physical health and fitness: **Poise**, **Aerobic Fitness**, **Flexibility**, and **Muscular Strength**. I will define and expand upon each one of these pillars, giving you both understanding and foundation exercises to help you toward success in each one of them.

the new science of body and mind

As the new century and new millennium dawn, all the research and psychological and medical health findings are confirming that those who are physically active score better across-the-board on all tests of mental skills than those who are unfit. If you test your mental skills when you are unfit, and then test them again, after having become very fit, you will find a significant overall improvement.

Similarly research has confirmed that the reverse of this is also true. The child who in general scores better in tests of mental skills is, on average, fitter, healthier and more emotionally well-adjusted and happy than the child whose mental skills test results are poor.

To round off the good news, the creative geniuses were once again found to be the opposite of what the public expected them to be. They were, and are, particularly robust, organized, energetic, vibrant, and physically fit and strong. They all also exhibited tremendous physical and mental stamina.

The picture is now complete: the Greeks and Romans were correct in espousing the principle of *mens sana in corpore sano*: a healthy mind in a healthy body.

It is becoming increasingly apparent that to study the brain as an organ separate from the body, and to study the body as a separate unit from the brain, is counterproductive. By doing so we lose the synergetic relationship between both, and thus miss out on more than 99 percent of the possible benefits (see the discussion on the **Brain Principle of Synergy**, pages 4–8). It is essential, therefore, to study each, both as itself and its biology and function, in relation with the other. We thus combine the studies of psychology, biology, anatomy, and physiology in the discipline of **Holanthropy**, introduced for the first time here in *Head Strong*. Holanthropy (from the Greek *holos*, meaning "whole" and *anthropos*, meaning a human being) is the study of precisely that: the whole human being. You!

In the following pages you will discover some amazing facts about of what and how you are made, and will realize just how fabulously interrelated *are* your body and brain.

Let's start with those amazing facts.

In the box that follows are just some of the facts about your body and brain that have been discovered recently, and which confirm that you are a walking miracle!

- Each human is created from a single sperm, one of four hundred million produced by their father, and a single egg produced by their mother. These eggs are so small that it would take two million to fill an acorn cup.
- Since the beginning time there have been 70 billion humans, each one astoundingly different from all the others.
- With the multiple genetic variations contained within each sperm and egg, there is the capability of creating 300 *trillion* humans beings, who are all genetically unique.
- Each human eye contains 130 million light receptors. Each light receptor can take in at least five photons (bundles of light energy) per second. The Cern Laboratory in Switzerland has estimated that it would take US$68,000,000-worth of equipment to duplicate just one of your eyes.
- Each human ear contains 24,000 fibers that are able to detect enormous ranges and subtle distinctions in the molecular vibrations of the air.

- The human olfactory system can identify the chemical odorant of an object in one part per trillion of air.
- To empower body movement, locomotion and environmental sensitivity, we each have 200 intricately architectured bones, 500 totally coordinated muscles, and seven miles of nerve fibers.
- The human heart beats on average 36,000,000 times each year, pumping an equivalent of 600,000 gallons of blood each year through 60,000 miles of tubing, arteries, veins and capillaries.
- Human lungs are composed of 600,000,000 globes of atmosphere-sensitive capacity.
- The blood circulating in the human body contains 22 trillion blood cells. Within each blood cell are millions of molecules, and within each molecule is an atom oscillating at more than 10 million times per second.
- Two million blood cells die each second. These are immediately replaced by two million more.
- The human brain contains a million million neurons or nerve cells.
- The human brain contains 1 trillion protein molecules.
- The number of internal "maps of thought" that the brain is capable of producing is one followed by 10.5 million kilometers of standard typewritten zeros.
- Each human body has four million pain-sensitive structures.
- Throughout the human body there are 500,000 touch sensors.
- Throughout the human body there are 200,000 temperature sensors.
- Within each human body there is enough atomic energy to build any of the world's greatest cities many times over.
- Research is increasingly showing that the creative and memory powers of the brain are infinite.
- Your mouth is the most sophisticated chemical laboratory the planet has ever known. It can distinguish, by using combinations of sweet, salt, sour and bitter taste sensations as well as odour, over a billion different tastes.

how to look after a human

Imagine that, at the age of 15, every human on the earth was given a box, in which was housed a most beautiful sculpture of a human being, and which contained the following instructions:

This sculpture is your umbilical cord to life, health and happiness. It is, literally, your Lifeline. Your sculpture is made of sensitive though incredibly resilient material. This material requires only 30 minutes per day of your time to maintain it in tip-top condition for 100 years. If it remains in tip-top condition, then so will you. Any deterioration in the sculpture will have an immediate and similarly deleterious effect on your own body. Your magical sculpture is beyond value. It is also irreplaceable - lose or destroy it and you die.

What do you think the reaction of the average human being would be to the sculpture?

They would obviously consider it the most valuable and precious possession on earth, would be in awe of its life-giving and life-taking powers, would spend time and fortunes maintaining and protecting it, and would treat it with the reverence it deserves.

It is *your* body that is the bastion, the protector, the transportation system, the nourisher and the provider for your brain. Maintain it as you would that sculpture, and it will maintain you. Neglect and abuse it, and you simply neglect and abuse your magical self.

The following pages deal with the different aspects of health, and give guidelines to help you maintain and improve your own health in the most enjoyable and effective ways.

But before we enter your "Physical Gym" let's first dispel some popular misconceptions.

myth-busting

MYTH: "Bright people (nerds) are unfit; fit people are thick!"
TRUTH: First, let's point out that this myth, common today, is based on the thinking of the last two centuries in which the human race has, metaphorically, disconnected its brain from its body! The world felt that intellectual health and physical health were not only not connected – they were actually *negatively* correlated: *the intelligent were weak and the strong were thick!*

It was only at the end of the 20th century that the breath-taking discovery was made that our brains are actually *connected* to our bodies! And not only connected - they are an integral and intricately associated duo: what affects one profoundly affects the other, as you will see throughout this and the next two chapters.

Remember: **If you exercise your brain you will positively influence your body; if you exercise your body you will positively influence your brain.** So, if you do ever meet a very fit athlete whom you consider to be not particularly intelligent, rest assured that if that individual were not an athlete, he or she would be even less intelligent!

The bright are strong and the strong are brighter!

MYTH: "Pure aerobics is all you need to stay fit."
TRUTH: Yes, you do need aerobics (see page 171). But you *also* need Poise, Flexibility and Strength if you are to be *truly* fit.

MYTH: "If you exercise you don't have to be so concerned with what you eat."
TRUTH: When you exercise you need to be even *more* concerned with what you eat.

This is a simple and obvious one. When you exercise, you are placing more demands on your body than normal. If your body is having demands placed on it, it needs to be completely prepared to meet those energy demands. If your nutrition is inadequate, then the body will not be able to respond to the exercise challenge, and in this depleted state will place itself at risk of damage or injury.

A good well-rounded diet is *essential* if you are to exercise well and to your maximum benefit.

MYTH: "Sex before exercise reduces the performance and the benefits of that exercise."
TRUTH: Happily, there is no evidence for this!

MYTH: "The longer you exercise the better."
TRUTH: For maximum benefit, your workouts should average between 20 minutes and an hour. Much more than this and you put an unnecessary strain on body and mind.

MYTH: "You are 'stuck' with your body type, so what's the point of trying to change it?"
TRUTH: Of course you are born with a body type; the point of fitness and health is not to try to "change" it – it is to develop and sculpt it!

You *can* transform your body!

The recent flowering of incredibly different forms of physical exercise and pursuits has demonstrated to us just how adaptable every body is. Consider the Sumo wrestler, the marathon runner, the bodybuilder, the anorexic, the "couch potato," the gymnast, and the mime. Each one demonstrates that by will and persistence the body, even more so than marble, can be sculpted to a desired (and sometimes undesired – remember 300-pound Tony!) form. Your body is adaptable, and simply awaits your proper care and development.

A high level of general fitness denotes freedom from disease, of course, and psychological well-being as well. Other components are also important. Reasonable muscular development, functional flexibility of the joints, adequate vital capacity of the lungs, reserved capacity of the heart and blood vessels, and stamina, must all be included. Stamina in this context means the capacity to endure exertion and stressful physical activity as a reflection of good cardio-pulmonary reserve."

Lt. General Richard L. Bohannon, Surgeon General, United States Air Force (ret.)

general physical fitness

There are four main columns to the temple of your physical fitness:

- poise
- aerobic training and fitness
- flexibility
- strength

1. poise

Poise is defined as *graceful and elegant bearing*, involving composure and dignity of manner. It is a state in which the individual is in balance; in equilibrium.

Each of the four areas of Poise, Aerobic Fitness, Flexibility and Strength is vitally important. However, if you perform the other three without poise, they can do you more harm than good; if you perform the other three with poise, they can do you a power of good!

Poise was once thought of as a state possessed by only a few "blessed" individuals; increasingly we have come to realize that it is a state natural to *all* individuals. This realization has come about primarily because of the work of Matthias Alexander, who introduced the world to the "Alexander Technique" of movement and posture, and who is increasingly regarded as one of the Great Brains of the 20th century.

His story is an intriguing one. As you read it, think about the implications of Alexander's findings to your own life and body.

an uplifting story

Matthias Alexander was born in Tasmania in 1869. Alexander was especially interested in Shakespeare, and after studying drama and performance began to do one-man shows on the Bard's work. His performances were excellent, and he began to build a reputation both for the power of his voice and projection, and for his overall performance and stage presence.

And then the trouble with his body began...

When he was comfortably into the middle section of his performances, Alexander found that his voice began to go hoarse, and by the end of his performances he was often in considerable discomfort.

As this condition was "career threatening," Alexander sought advice from drama teachers, voice trainers, and doctors. He was prescribed potions, lotions, pills, balms, a change of air, and rest. Alexander tried the various remedies, but infuriatingly, at about the same point in each of his performances, the hoarseness returned.

Eventually an especially important performance loomed on the horizon. Alexander consulted the leading doctor in the field, and was advised to give his body and voice a complete two-week rest before the performance. This he dutifully took.

And in the performance?

At the same point his hoarseness returned.

Alexander furiously confronted his doctor, only to be advised to take even more rest. Concluding that all the experts must be missing the point, Alexander decided to become his own doctor.

He had noticed that in conversations with friends and colleagues, he could discuss, debate, and lower and raise the volume of his voice for hours on end, with *no hoarseness whatsoever*. Surely, Alexander reasoned, the reason for the hoarseness during performances must be something that he was doing with

2. Your *lung capacity* will be significantly reduced. This will force you to take short, gasping breaths, thus supplying less vital oxygen to your body and brain.

3. Your *cardiovascular system*. In a slouched position most of your major arteries and blood vessels will be constricted. It is as if you were putting multiple clamps on all the major "tubes" of your blood supply system. This also puts an extra strain and tension on your heart, which has to pump harder in order to force your blood through.

4. Your *nerves*. As with the blood, a cramped and slouched posture pinches the nerves, slowing down the transmission of essential "Nerve Knowledge" and often causing pain in the process (sciatica, the shooting pains at the base of the spine and down the back of the legs is often caused by mis-aligned poise).

5. Your *muscles* have to work much harder to keep you in position if your balance is "off kilter."

Similarly, if your body is off balance when you are involved in any aerobic activity, then discomfort and injury will be the probable eventual outcomes. Obviously, exactly the same is true for any muscular lifting, pulling or pushing activity or weight training.

Nor do you have to be very active for inappropriate poise to cause serious injury – standing in high-heels is another example! Being forced into this unnatural position produces the following undesirable changes:

1. The *pelvis*. Your body is designed to balance over a stable base – your feet. If this balance is pushed forward, the body compensates by tilting the pelvis unnaturally.

2. The *spine*. With the body's natural point of balance out of alignment, the spine can, over time, also be thrown out of alignment.

3. The *back*. Because of the mis-alignment of the spine, serious lower back problems, one of the most common problems among women today, are much more likely.

4. The *calf*. In high-heels calf muscles tighten and shorten. They become less functional.

5. The *knee*. Because of the tight calf muscle and forward position of the body, considerable extra stress is placed on the rest of the leg, especially the knee joint. Injury is likely.

6. The *foot*. The foot is one of the most delicate and magnificently designed parts of your body. High-heels, literally, begin to destroy it. With a two-inch heel 150 percent of a woman's weight is pushed directly onto the ball of her foot; with a three-inch heel, *double* the woman's weight is pushed onto the ball of the foot! This creates huge tensions in the tendons of the feet, making the ankle unstable. It also distorts the ball of the foot and toes, leading to hard skin, calluses, cramp, cycles of pain, and deformity of the bones.

Poise is important!

An interesting story about a tough marathon runner will make the point, and will serve as a wonderful example and role model for you.

paul the marathon runner and his "feet of blood"

By 1952 Paul Collins, then aged 26, had set the Canadian marathon world record, had run the New York Marathon, and had become the Canadian National Marathon Champion and record-holder, and had qualified for the Helsinki Olympics in that year. He had a reputation as one of the prodigies in the marathon field, and was known as a particularly tough runner who could break through most of the pain barriers experienced by marathoners.

The 1952 marathon in Helsinki was a particularly difficult one, and Collins' competition was very high class. By the beginning of the second half of the race his feet were already beginning to blister, and his muscles and joints to ache.

He ran on. Through the pain.

As the race entered its final stages, Collins was in the leading group, and fighting bravely on. By this time his muscles and joints were screaming in agony, and his feet were beginning to bleed.

Still he pushed himself onward.

In the final two miles the pain was almost unbearable. Collins endured it.

He pushed and pushed, his energy being drained by the length of the race, his excruciating agonies, and the loss of blood from his feet, which had now, as he described it, become "crimson pads."

Collins, being Collins, finished the race. His position? A very creditable 19th.

And then came the horrifying aftermath ... In the days after the event, Paul Collins' body gradually seized up. Doctors told him that he had seriously overdone it; that his legs, their tendons, joints and muscles were severely damaged; that he would never run again; and that he was, from that time on, a semi-cripple. For years he had to live with that verdict, hardly able to crawl upstairs, and walking with pronounced limps. Even rising from a chair was a painful experience.

He came to accept that the "hardness" of the run had indeed been the cause of his misfortune. And then, Collins reported to me, one day he had a sudden life-changing revelation. He realized that the 18 runners who had beaten him in the marathon had continued to run in major competitions after the Helsinki Olympics. *And they had all run faster and "harder" than he had!* It was therefore not the speed of the race or the toughness of the course that had caused his injuries. It must be something else. That something else could only be the *way* in which he had run that race; the *way* in which he had used (and as he eventually discovered, *misused*) himself during the race.

Like Alexander, Collins began to examine his use of his body, and found that, sure enough, all his injuries could be related to the way in which his poor poise had enabled his own brain to use his body, unnecessarily, to pound parts of itself during extreme exertion.

He continued his intensive studies, including the Alexander Technique, and trained himself to walk with more elegance and grace. By the age of 35 he was walking longer distances. A few years later he was beginning, gently, to run again, using the Good New Habit of his improved bodily alignment. Within a couple more years he was running up to 10 miles; and a few years after that he ran his first "poised" marathon.

Being the great experimenter he was, Collins extended himself further, exploring the realms of the ultra marathon. Between the ages of 55 through 60, he set world records for his age group for the 200, 300 and 400-mile runs; for the 200, 300 and 400-kilometer runs; plus 3, 4, 5 and 6-day records at the third annual 6-day race in Nottingham, England.

At the age of 60 he entered a 24-hour race (in which you run for as long as you can, rest, and then continue, for 24 hours; your distances covered being measured constantly by judges around the track).

In 24 hours, including breaks, how far do you think Collins ran?

He established a new United Kingdom all-comers' record by covering 117 miles, the distance of nearly *five* marathons in the time!

At the end of such ultra marathon events the finish line is festooned with doctors, physiotherapists, masseurs and all manner of people lined up to deal with the results of the extreme physical strains and stresses to which the bodies of the competitors have been put. It became a laughing point at such finishing lines that when Collins, still maintaining his superb running poise, was asked what he needed, he would reply, "Only a pint of beer, thank you!"

One sidelight of Paul Collins' career is that he helped me with mine! Due to my own bad poise, I injured my lower back in the gym by lifting heavy weights while I was not properly balanced. I had been told by many experts (much as Alexander himself was told concerning his voice) that there was no real cure to the constant and nagging pain I had in my lower back, because I had irreversibly damaged it.

I was eventually advised to go to Paul Collins, who was teaching proper alignment, poise and how to move and run with the Alexander Technique at that time.

By showing me some of the horrendous Big Bad Physical Habits into which

I had allowed my posture to degenerate, he demonstrated that much of my discomfort and pain was because of the constant pressure my body was putting on itself. By helping me to realign myself, Collins guided me to complete freedom from pain, and to the re-emergence of my running and physical career, which had been suspended for over a year.

In summary, we see that perfect *poise* is the perfect *balance* of the body, in which all aspects of your muscular, organic and skeletal systems are properly aligned. Of particular importance are the relative positioning of your head, neck, spine and joints. It is possible to be aerobically, flexibly and muscularly fit, yet still to be "off balance." This is why poise forms the first column in your temple of general physical fitness.

Proper poise allows fluidity of movement, and a natural flow of all energies throughout your bodily systems. This is often described as a "balanced resting state," in which the body, no matter what its position, is fundamentally alert and ready to spring effectively into action from non-action, and into other action from any existing action. One of the best examples of this is a cat.

Another example of perfect poise in action is the champion athlete/physical performer. Such individuals are typically described in terms such as "graceful," "elegant," "natural," "free," and "refined." These words are the brain's *natural* reaction to seeing others in their natural state of poise.

One outstanding example of this is the Jamaican sprinter, Merlene Ottey. She has been sprinting in national, regional, world and Olympic championships for over 20 years, in a sport in which the lifetime of the athlete is usually very short. Unlike other sprinters she has been surprisingly free of injury throughout her career. Why? Because she is one of the few who runs with superb body

Figure 23: good posture

alignment, thus reducing drastically the chance of injury every time she trains or runs in competition.

It is significant that Merlene is renowned not only for the elegance and grace of her running, but for her positive thinking. There is a very close correlation between the two, as you will discover in the Poise Workout.

Good poise is a major key to your maintaining and developing your physical fitness and health. It also has wider, social implications.

Michael J. Gelb, one of the world's leading Poise and Alexander teachers, tells of the following interesting research on poise and its effect on other people.

Two groups of people, convicted pickpockets and dance and poise teachers, were asked to observe films of people walking down New York streets.

The pickpockets were asked to rate the people on a scale of zero to 10. Zero indicated someone so "pickpocketable" that even if the pickpocket had sworn never to pick another pocket again, this person would be so tempting that the vow would be broken. A score of 10 indicated that even if the pickpocket and his family were starving, this person would still be deemed too great a risk.

The dance and poise teachers were asked to rank the people similarly. A score of zero indicated that the person was completely and utterly off balance and lacking in poise. A score of 10 indicated perfect poise.

When the two sets of scores were compared, there was a positive correlation of over 80 percent between the degree of a person's pickpocketability and their lack of poise and balance!

Regardless of strength, looks, size or weight, pickpockets accurately sensed that, no matter what the other variables were, if the person were well balanced, it represented far more risk.

Now that you are more aware of the great importance and impact of poise for your personal physical fitness and health, how do you maintain and improve yours? Find out in the Poise Workout!

poise workout

1. be aware of your poise

Develop an appropriate awareness of the relative excellence of your poise in your everyday activities such as walking, running, sitting down, standing up, bending, lifting, eating, brushing your teeth, talking on the telephone, listening, driving the car, and especially during all forms of physical exercise. Run through in your mind the following checklist:

- Am I slouching?
- Am I stiffening my neck?
- Am I pulling my head back/slumping it forward?
- Am I raising my shoulders unnecessarily?
- Am I locking any joints?
- Am I thrusting my hips forward and the small of my back inward?
- Is my breathing deep, free and rhythmical or shallow, gaspy and "held?"

Whenever you notice that your alignment could be improved, don't immediately readjust it by using your old habits of thinking. Pause for a moment, and then use Alexander's Primary Control posture - making sure that your neck is free, then that your head is "up," and then that your back is open and wide. When Primary Control is in place, specifically focus on any areas of tension, your joints and your breathing.

Remember – Think Body!

2. find "good poise" role models

Be on the look out for examples of people or animals demonstrating excellent poise. Regularly imprint these images in your brain, and you will be building up a **Good New Habit** of Poise Visions. Allow yourself to become poised, like them.

You may find it helpful to photocopy pictures of poised people or animals, such as dancers or big cats, and place them where they will be a constant reminder of the type of poise that has become your goal.

3. use the success formula TEFCAS

Copy Alexander, and stand in front of a mirror, and simply look at the creature in front of you. Objectively, **Check** what you see. Is your head perfectly aligned or is it tilted in any direction on top of your spine? Is one shoulder higher than the other (in most people one is!)? Do your arms hang by your sides evenly? Are any of your joints "locked?"

When your senses have received this **Feedback** and your brain has **Checked**, pause, and allow, as Alexander did, your natural "Perfect Poise" to reintroduce itself.

4. take up a "good poise" hobby

Consider taking up a new hobby or hobbies that encourage good poise. Excellent disciplines for helping you to attain poise include certain forms of dance and yoga, Aikido and, especially, the Alexander Technique.

5. voice/poise practice

Practice, again in front of the mirror, reading to yourself. Listen intently to the sound of your own voice. Carry on reading as you tilt your head in different directions, constrict or open your neck and throat muscles, slouch, stand rigidly erect, take short breaths and generally experiment with every postural variation you can. Make it a fun game. Throughout, listen to the change in your voice, and, once again using the **Success Formula TEFCAS**, get your **Feedback**, **Check** it and continually **Adjust** towards **Success**. This is a wonderful exercise to try with family or friends.

6. use gravity to pull you through

On a daily basis, let gravity be your chiropractor, Alexander teacher, relaxation coach and guide. Perform the Poise Lying Down exercise below, which is designed, with the help of gravity, to straighten out the kinks and mis-alignments that may have accrued through your everyday activities. All you need for this little exercise is a relatively quiet place, some comfortable floor space, a one- to-two-inch thick book, and 5-10 minutes. The procedure is as follows:

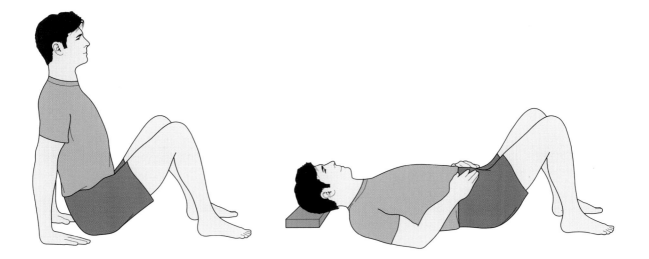

Figure 24: lying down poise exercise

(a) Begin by placing the book on the floor. Stand facing away from the book, approximately your body's length from it, with your feet shoulder-width apart. Allow your hands to rest gently at your sides, feeling the weight of gravity, and look straight ahead. Pause for a few moments checking your poise, breathing and that your joints are unlocked.

(b) Think of Primary Control, allowing your neck to be free so that your head can go forward and up and your entire torso can lengthen and widen. Breathing freely, become aware of the contact of your feet on the floor and notice, especially if you are standing in front of a mirror, the distance of your feet to the top of your head. Keep your eyes opened and alert, and listen to the sounds around you.

(c) Moving easily and elegantly, bend your ankle, knee and hip joints as you crouch down to sit on the floor. Exhale as you do this. Supporting yourself with your hands behind you, place your feet on the floor in front of you with your knees bent, while you continue to breath easily. Another way of getting to the floor is to first put one leg back, and then bend the knee so that you are in a kneeling position similar to as if you were about to be Knighted! From this gently get yourself into a sitting position and continue.

(d) Let your head continue to go forward and up to ensure that you are not tightening up your neck muscles and pulling your head back. Then, gently roll your spine back along the floor like a rolled rug unfurling, so that you end up with your head resting on the book. The book should be positioned so it supports your head at the place where your neck ends and your head begins. The purpose of the book is to allow gravity gradually to lengthen your neck while you lie in the position. Make sure that the height of the book is not so high that it stretches your neck unduly, and not so low that the neck is not given an opportunity to extend.

In this position your feet remain flat on the floor, with your knees pointing up to the ceiling and your hands resting gently on your chest. Allow the weight of your body to be fully supported by the floor.

(e) Once you are in this position, all you need to do is to allow your teacher and guide, gravity, to do its work. As you rest, gravity will be lengthening your spine, letting your organs exist in the full space of your torso, realigning that torso, allowing your breathing to become more deep and easy, straightening your shoulders, and allowing your neck to extend and be free.

(f) Check each part of your body, and especially be aware of the floor supporting your entire back, as it "melts" into a greater lengthening and widening.

(g) As you perform the exercise, you may also repeat to yourself some of your Brain Boosters, using this opportunity to build up your **Meta-Positive** Good New Thinking and Postural Habits. During this exercise it is often a good idea to keep your eyes open, as this keeps you alert and will prevent you from dozing off! However, should you wish to close your eyes, feel free to do so.

(h) After you have rested, and you feel your body is now more aligned, you are ready to stand up again. This should be done gracefully and elegantly too, being careful as you return to standing to maintain the opened and lengthened posture that gravity has helped you to establish.

In order to achieve a smooth transition from the exercise to standing, first decide when you are going to move, then gently roll over on to your front, maintaining your new sense of integration, expansion and poise. Ease your way into a crawling position, then go up onto one knee, with your head leading the movement up, and return to a standing position.

Don't immediately rush back into your previous postural habits! Pause for a moment, and sense where you are. Once again, feel your feet on the floor, and notice the distance between your feet and the top of your head. You may be surprised to discover that that distance has expanded! Check your new postural alignment, and reintegrate your breathing. As you gracefully move into the ongoing activities of your life, think about maintaining the new poise and posture that your friend gravity has helped put back into its "proper place."

7. imagination and your body

For a dramatic demonstration of the effect of mood and positive/negative thinking on posture, act out, using your full *imaginative powers*, the following two scenarios.

(a) Sit down in front of a mirror, and imagine that it has been one of the worst days of your life. As you imagine each of the horrible things that have happened, act out, dramatically, how someone's posture would adjust to each successive piece of news. In this day you discover:

   (i)   that you have just gone bankrupt
   (ii)   that you have an illness that will put you out of action for a year
   (iii) that the person you love most does not love you
   (iv)   that your best friend has just lied to and cheated you
   (v)   that you have been fired
   (vi)   that your favourite team has just lost a Final
   (vi)   that the weather forecast is awful!

When you are in the final posture, continue to think about these horrible events as if they were true, allow the posture to deteriorate even further if appropriate, and check, step-by-step, every part of you. Check how each part feels, and how efficiently it can function in its current position. Check also your energy levels and your desire to create and solve problems.

You should, in this state, and in all senses of the word, be de-pressed. Your thoughts have had a total and transformative effect on your entire body. Your thoughts have been **Meta-Negative**. They have totally dominated your physical and mental poise.

(b) Imagine next that it has been the best day of your life. As you imagine each successive piece of good news, once again act out how your body would respond.

   (i)   you have just been told you have won the lottery
   (ii)   your doctor says that you are in the best health of your life and are in the top 1 percent of fit people
   (iii) the person whom you love and whom you are not sure loves you, tells you that they have loved you in secret for years and thinks that you are the most amazing person they have ever met
   (iv)   your best friend confirms, by a series of actions, total dedication and support for you
   (v)   you are promoted at work to the position of which you have always dreamed
   (vi)   your favourite team wins the Cup
   (vii) the short and long-range weather forecasts are exactly what you desire!

At the end of this exercise, if you are still sitting, you will in all probability be radiantly upright with your body, senses and mind all blazingly open. If you have acted it well you will probably be like someone who has just won a world championship, with your arms raised and every part of you perfectly "up" and aligned!

You have been thinking **Meta-Positively**!

From this exercise you can see that one of the most important factors in the development of your Perfect Poise is the internal state of your thinking. Think poorly and that poor thinking is reflected in Poor Poise; think well and your poise naturally flourishes.

Following are some Brain Boosters that will help you achieve **Good New Habits** in your thinking, and which will automatically help improve your poise. They are double-whammy Brain Boosters because they contain thoughts which, in addition to being **Meta-Positive**, are directly related to the improvement of your bodily alignment.

brain boosters

1. My body's positions and movements are increasingly aligned, graceful, flowing and easy.
2. I am allowing my neck to be free so that my head may go forward and up and my back may lengthen and widen.
3. My breathing is relaxed, deep, open and free. I regularly mimic those people and animals demonstrating beautiful poise.
4. I am regularly in a state of relaxed awareness and concentration.

2. aerobic training and fitness

At the beginning of the 21st century 14,000 children aged between 8 and 12 participated in a study to trace the effects of exercise on academic performance. The study concluded that those pupils who do regular exercise do better in the "three Rs." Those who took part in a sport or vigorous activity three times a week were more likely to get good scores in their examinations.

One of the findings of the study, for example, found that 79 percent of boys who scored above average marks in national English tests also exercised at least three times a week. Of those children who scored below average, only 38 percent exercised for the same period.

Angela Balding, who led this study, said:

There's a definite link between those who are active three or four times a week and those youngsters who do better in the classroom. The research that is going into brain activity at the moment suggests that the reason may be that in those kids who are active, more oxygen gets to their brains. Their brains are then better equipped to take more in and be receptive to new things.

an array of exercise/health studies

- Research carried out at Queen's University, Belfast and Glasgow University has shown that one in three people are at risk from having a heart attack because they do not take sufficient cardiovascular exercise.
- A study of 13,000 people over a period of eight years, undertaken by the American Heart Association, found that those in the least fit group had a mortality rate three times higher than those in the fittest group.
- Brigham and Women's Hospital in Boston, Massachusetts studied 85,000 women over a period of 14 years. They concluded that an hour's exercise a day can cut the chances of breast cancer by up a fifth.
- At Chang Gung University in Taiwan, researchers found that men who exercised regularly had an 83 percent lower risk of developing colon cancer than sedentary men.

Men who exercise five or more times a week have been identified as having a 42% lower risk of developing diabetes than those who exercise less frequently.

The Times, Saturday, November 25, 2000

the discovery of a new fitness!

In the second part of the 20th century, a major new discovery was made concerning the nature of real physical fitness.

The story concerns a young and brilliant medical doctor, Dr. Kenneth Cooper. A considerable athlete/runner himself, Dr. Cooper had graduated from the Harvard School of Public Health, and was working at the United States Air Force School of Aerospace Medicine in Texas.

In the middle of the 1960s Dr. Cooper began his investigations into "what really is physical fitness and health?" His studies involved more than 25,000 individuals, including officers and airmen, pilots and astronauts, athletes and non-athletes, the active and the inactive, the healthy and the unhealthy, women and men. It was one of the largest research projects ever attempted in the field of physical conditioning.

The studies provided cascades of information and data on how to exercise, the type of exercise, and how the presence or lack of exercise affects on the human body. The research showed that traditional thoughts about what constitutes a healthy and fit body had missed a vital component: *Aerobic Conditioning*. Aerobics refers to any exercise that stimulates heart and lung activity for a time period sufficiently long to produce significant and beneficial changes in the body. Typical aerobic exercises include fast walking, running, swimming, cycling and rowing.

Aerobic training builds up your stamina and endurance by forcing your heart to pump more life-giving and oxygen-carrying blood to all the muscles and organs of your body - including your brain.

Aerobic fitness is an overall fitness often called "endurance fitness" or "working capacity" - your ability to do prolonged work without undue fatigue. It has some connection with your body's muscular strength, and *much* more connection with your body's *overall* health, the health of your heart, lungs, entire cardiovascular system and all your other organs, including your muscles.

the "training effect"

When you train aerobically, the training causes changes in the various systems and organs of your body. This is called the "training effect." The exercise has to be of sufficient intensity and duration to oblige your body to make changes to deal with the extra effort you are asking it to make.

Aerobic exercise specifically produces a training effect that increases the ability of your body to utilize oxygen.

1. It improves the size, strength and pumping efficiency of your heart. This means that with each beat, more blood can be pumped around your body. This improves your ability to transport life-sustaining oxygen from your lungs to your heart and ultimately to all other parts of your body.
2. It strengthens your breathing muscles. This tends to reduce the resistance to air flow, making breathing easier, and ultimately facilitates the rapid flow of air in and out of your lungs.
3. It tones up the muscles throughout your body. This improves your general circulation, can lower your blood pressure, and reduces the workload on your heart.
4. It produces an increase in the total amount of blood circulating in your body and makes your blood a more efficient oxygen carrier.

In summary, it is the *inside of your body* that needs to be fit, and this is accomplished by increasing its ability to take in one of its main "fuels" – oxygen.

Oxygen is very different from your other main source of physical energy – nutrition/food – because, unlike food, oxygen cannot be stored. Therefore, you need to replenish your oxygen supply constantly, which is why we inhale and exhale every minute of our lives.

You might think, then, that all you would need to do to get in more oxygen is simply to breathe more! But this is not the case. If your system is restricted and unhealthy, it simply does not have the capacity to get enough oxygen to all the necessary areas - those nearly infinite areas and extremities of your body where the food is stored. When the oxygen *does* meet the stored food, the two combine to produce the energy that is so essential to your health, fitness and survival.

Even when your body is minimally active, such as when it is sleeping, it is constantly bringing in a supply of oxygen to help burn the foodstuffs that give you energy to survive through the night. When you are sleeping you still require energy for your heart to continue beating, for your circulation system to do its ongoing jobs of maintenance and repair, for your digestive system to function, for all your chemical balances to be maintained, for your body temperature to be held steady, and for your lungs to bring in even more energy to keep the process (i.e., you!) alive.

In this state, you are operating at *minimum* requirements. For the aerobically unfit person, *minimum* requirements are very close to their *maximum* capacity! For the aerobically fit person, the body can very easily handle minimum requirements, and can similarly handle with relative ease activities that become increasingly more vigorous.

How is it you attain the wonderful idea of excellent aerobic fitness, and is there a formula for doing so? There is!

the correct aerobic formula

The correct aerobic formula is exceptionally simple, easy to apply and will provide you with significant all-round improvement in your health and vitality.

To become and stay aerobically fit (oxygen fit) you need to exercise only four times a week, for a minimum of 30 minutes a time (even less than you had to spend on your magic sculpture!)

Forms of exercise that particularly help you become aerobically fit, and which, when you do them well, are extremely enjoyable and satisfying, include swimming, fast and long-distance walking, running, cross-country skiing, dancing, rowing, making love, and using the growing range of aerobic training machines that mimic a number of these activities.

Each exercise session should start with a five-minute warm-up, followed by 20 minutes of hard aerobic fitness training, followed by a five-minute cool-down and stretching period. The warm-up period ensures that your body will be "revved up" for the exercise to come. The cool-down period guarantees a smooth transition between hard exercise and your normal activity.

When you maintain hard aerobic training for at least 20 minutes, a constant message is sent to your brain and body that they are in danger of running out of oxygen. This is life threatening! As a result, a "red alert" message goes out to all systems, instructing them to "crank up" in order to deal with the increased demands. This is why doing the activity for at least 20 minutes is so vital. If you train for only 10-15 minutes per session, your brain and body will say to themselves something like "Oh, this is a little bit difficult, but it's not going to last for long. No need to change."

It is this phenomenal ability of your system to adjust itself to the stresses and strains being placed on it that is the basis of aerobic training, and as you will see in the Strength Building section of this chapter, muscular development training.

During the time of hard aerobic training, your heart should maintain a pulse rate of between 120-180 beats per minute (depending upon your age and current physical condition). The aerobic conditioning exercises should ideally be done every other day, and can comfortably be alternated with poise, flexibility and strength training.

When you are engaged in aerobic exercise, the following table will give you a general guide to pulse rates that are reached at increasing intensities of effort:

scale of perceived exertion	pulse rate
1 – Very, very light	Under 90
2 – Very light	90
3 – Light	100
4 – Fairly light	110
5 – Neither light nor heavy ("moderate")	120
6 – Somewhat heavy	130
7 – Heavy	140
8 – Very heavy	150
9 – Very, very heavy	160

The effects of even this modest amount of exercise on your body and brain are astonishing.

body workout equals brain workout

Rodney Swain and his colleagues at the University of Wisconsin in Milwaukee have come up with some remarkable findings about the speed with which the brain adapts positively to exercise, regardless of age.

Studies had previously shown that young animals sprout blood vessels in the brain after bursts of exercise. The suspicion was that this was only possible early in life. To test the truth of this, Swain and his colleagues tested middle-aged rats, some of whom did, and some whom did not do "rat aerobics."

The rats that declined to take exercise showed no change in their brains. The rats that had done aerobics showed a dramatic increase in the density of blood vessels in the regions of their brains connected to exercise. The astonishing thing about this finding was that *"all the growth had taken place within three days of initiating aerobic activity,"* Swain said. *"It shows that the brain can make rapid changes to its oxygen supply."*

Swain suggests that because the neurons in the motor (physical) cortex and cerebellum are stepping up activity in conjunction with the exercise, they need more nutrients and oxygen. Noting this need, the brain uses the extra energy from the aerobic exercise to sprout extra capillaries to supply the extra nutrients and oxygen in the newly working areas of the brain.

Interestingly, in the context of *Head Strong*, Swain speculates that cognitive workouts (thinking and Mind Sport activities) will probably also encourage the formation of new blood vessels to the "thinking areas" of the brain.

Encouragingly, the animals who had shown this increase also, of choice, began to run up to three times farther each day, suggesting that the brain and the body were both cooperating in guaranteeing the supply of more of this new "drug" – healthy blood!

bright and strong methuselahs

Exciting new research published in January 2001 has confirmed and extended previous research confirming the positive relationship between exercise and mental performance. Dr. James Blumathal and his colleagues at Duke University Medical Center in North Carolina computed that half-an-hour of aerobic activity three times a week was sufficient to bring about a significant increase in brainpower. In the experiment, it was confirmed that such exercise can boost memory and can help combat the effects of aging. Indeed, the improvements in mental and general performance were especially marked for the middle-aged and elderly.

Other of the so called "executive functions" of the brain which were also improved included planning, organization, and the ability to juggle with different intellectual tasks at the same time. (It was noted that inability in these areas is one of the main causes of stress.)

Another plus from the experiment was the fact that the improvements in performance were both *immediate* and *long-lasting*.

how aerobic training can transform the inner you

the effect of aerobics on your brain

The prime beneficiary of your aerobic fitness is your **brain** - remember, *mens sana in corpore sano*!

With every beat of your heart, blood is pumped directly into your brain. Bearing in mind the fact that your brain weighs only between 2 and 3 percent of your body weight, and that many of the capillaries that carry blood to it are microscopically small, what percentage of the blood do you think goes directly into your brain with every beat of your heart:

Less than 1 percent?

2-3 percent?

4-6 percent?

7-9 percent?

10 percent?

10-14 percent?

15-20 percent?

20-40 percent?

40-80 percent?

The answer, astonishingly, 20-40 percent!

The *entire* remainder of your bodily systems receive only just over half of the remaining blood resources! Nature considers your brain to be by far the most important part of you.

This is most dramatically demonstrated in severe crises. When a person has a major limb severed, the common assumption has been that most of the blood from each heartbeat will gush from that limb. Nothing could be further from the truth. The minute that the limb is severed, the entire brain and body system go into total emergency-aligned action. All the blood vessels of the severed limb immediately constrict in order to minimize blood loss. Simultaneously, the heart blasts the brain with even more blood than usual! Why? Because in this life-and-death situation, the *only* organ that is going to possibly save you is your brain. Nature therefore provides it with the greatest supplies of energy.

Aerobic exercise will increase the quality of your **sleep** and will often lessen the amount you require.

In another seminal study conducted by Dr. Cooper, two groups of subjects stay in bed, flat on their backs, for three full weeks. The first group exercised three times daily on bicycle ergometers strapped to their beds, while the other group was allowed no exercise.

The results: the exercise group had normal sleep patterns throughout, sleeping seven to eight hours a night. The group that was not allowed to exercise slept erratically, or occasionally developed a chronic insomnia. In a finding that appeared to go against common sense (but is predictable if you know about the nature of your body and brain), the group who had not exercised actually wanted to sleep for *longer*. When they were awake after having had more sleep than the other group, they were still comparatively listless. The aerobically trained group slept less *and* were more alert during the day.

When you are aerobically fit you give your brain a deeper and more meaningful rest and integrating period for *one quarter to one third of every day*. The remaining 66-75 percent of the day is then spent in a state of higher sensory and intellectual alertness and awareness.

the psychological effects of aerobic training

Because of the **Holanthropic** and intimate connection between the brain and body, physical fitness can now be seen to be in many ways equivalent to mental fitness.

A definite relationship has been found between physical fitness and mental alertness and emotional stability. In the first place, improved endurance performance makes the body less susceptible to fatigue, and consequently less likely to commit errors, mental or physical. Your performance can be sustained longer without the necessity for too frequent breaks.

Dr. Kenneth Cooper, United States Air Force School of Aerospace Medicine

This relates directly to the qualities of energy, stamina, persistence and focus of the great geniuses.

Dr. Appleton and Dr. Kobes at the United States Military Academy at West Point made a study that directly compared the physical aptitude and health of their cadets and their success at the Academy. Over four years, the cadets who were fit had an attrition rate half that of their unfit classmates. The drop-out rate was especially high among non-athletes, who found themselves incapable of absorbing the academic curriculum simply because they did not have the alertness and stamina to maintain the necessary mental effort.

Similar tests have shown highly positive correlations between performances in physical tests and exercises, and academic and leadership qualities. They have also revealed a positive correlation between physical health and mental outlook. People who are in good aerobic condition tend to be more self-confident, more optimistic, more determined, and generally have a greater love of their jobs and professions, a generally higher energy level, and a greater lust for life.

...such skepticism [about the "feel good factor" of exercise] all but evaporated following a wave of studies showing that exercise contributes to feelings of happiness, euphoria, calmness, and tranquility for anything from a few minutes to 24 hours.

New Scientist magazine, November 23, 1996

aerobic exercise and psychological "wellness"

A seminal study in this area was done at St. George's Hospital Medical School in London at the end of the 20th century. Andrew Steptoe and his colleagues worked with 109 sedentary adults who were randomly assigned to one of four groups. Each group was given a different exercise regime:

1. The first group did either moderate or high intensity aerobic training three times a week.
2. The second group did exactly the same.
3. The third group, instead of aerobics, did gentle stretching exercises.
3. The fourth group did nothing.

After 12 weeks the only two groups to show a significant improvement in psychological wellness were the aerobic trainers. Their tension, anxiety and confusion were all reduced. In addition there was a marked increase in how they perceived their ability to cope with stressful situations.

the effects of aerobic training on your body

The first effect of good aerobic training is that it increases the size and strength of your body's most important muscle – your **heart**. When the heart is strong and healthy, it is more efficient, and pumps, with less effort, more blood with each beat. Your stronger heart will be able to feed itself a stronger supply of nutrients, blood and oxygen, which makes it even stronger, which allows it to become physically more powerful and to supply even better nutrients, and so on in a positive synergetic spiral of health.

When your heart is healthy it will beat at 60 beats per minute or less, whereas when your heart is unfit it will beat at 80 or more beats per minute.

The mortality rate for men and women with pulse rates over 92 beats per minute at rest is four times greater than for those with pulse rates less than 67 beats per minute.

Dr. Laurence Morehouse, Professor of Exercise Physiology, University of California at Los Angeles

A heart that is unexercised is smaller, weak – like any unexercised muscle – and possesses smaller chambers into which the blood flows and from which it is pumped out. It is obvious that if your heart is weaker, unhealthy and therefore pumping less and less efficient blood, it will have to do far more work than if it is healthy. Paradoxically, the more you "work out" your heart, through a health-giving aerobic training programme, the less work your heart has to do.

The ability of your **lungs** to function and to supply your body with the much-needed oxygen is entirely dependent upon the "breathing fitness" of the muscles of your rib cage and diaphragm. These "breathing muscles" can get fit *only* by aerobic training. They also obviously work better if you are physically poised!

The statistics on "fit" versus "unfit" are eye-opening: an aerobically fit person can process *twice* as much oxygen in any given time period as an unfit person. When they are healthy, your lungs will also expel wastes and poisons from your body with a far greater efficiency. It is obvious from this that aerobic training has significant effects on the *amount* and *quality* of your **blood**, and on the arteries, veins and capillaries that supply it to all parts and organs of your body.

In conjunction with producing a bigger and healthier heart, your aerobically trained body will produce more blood, and within that blood more oxygen-carrying hemoglobin, more red blood cells to carry the hemoglobin, and more blood plasma for the red blood cells. In addition to these benefits, when you become aerobically fit, the total supply of blood in your cardiovascular system is considerably increased.

Studies have shown that in an average-sized man the blood volume in the body and brain will increase by as much as a quart in response to aerobic conditioning. At the same time the *quality* of the blood improves: each pint of blood will contain more red blood cells, meaning that the density of oxygen in your blood will be greater. This increased volume of hemoglobin allows more oxygen to be delivered to *all* parts of your body (including, especially, your brain), and more waste to be carried away.

Because in aerobic exercise, your whole body is usually exercised, your **muscles** will benefit as well. Obvious benefits such as muscle speed and endurance are supplemented by an improved muscle tone. When your muscles are aerobically fit they tend to be leaner, finer and longer than when they are untrained. This is because the additional capillaries created by your aerobic fitness surround more of each muscle fiber, feeding it more and taking away unnecessary poisons and fats.

When you are aerobically fit your entire **digestive system** will be more regularly oxygenated and cleansed. Conditions such as hyper-acidity will tend to decline and hormonal levels will balance out. As a result, all nutrition that is ingested will be more effectively processed.

High intensity aerobic training, particularly when it is combined with strength training, will strengthen your **bones** too. Because we only come into contact with "dead bones" we have developed globally two **Meta-Negative Thinking Habits** about them:

1. Our bones are brittle
2. They become very fragile with age

Your bones are in fact incredibly flexible, and are more like super-strong silicon. They will bend a very long way and withstand incredible pressure before breaking. If you exercise them aerobically and with weight resistance, they remain incredibly resilient throughout your life. It seems that this is because near maximum cardiovascular exercise stimulates the increased production of your human growth hormone. This can significantly increase cell function, assist protein synthesis and, while increasing muscle size and function, promote bone growth.

3. flexibility

Flexibility is the third of the four main columns of your body's temple. When you are becoming poised and aerobically fit, you will at the same time be increasing your flexibility. Flexibility exercises are excellent for the warm-up and cool-down periods.

Flexibility fitness refers to the ability of your body's joints to move freely in all the directions for which they were designed. For a masterful demonstration of just how flexible your joints can be, just watch any baby. This is a state in which your own body once was. It is only by applying the synergetically wrong

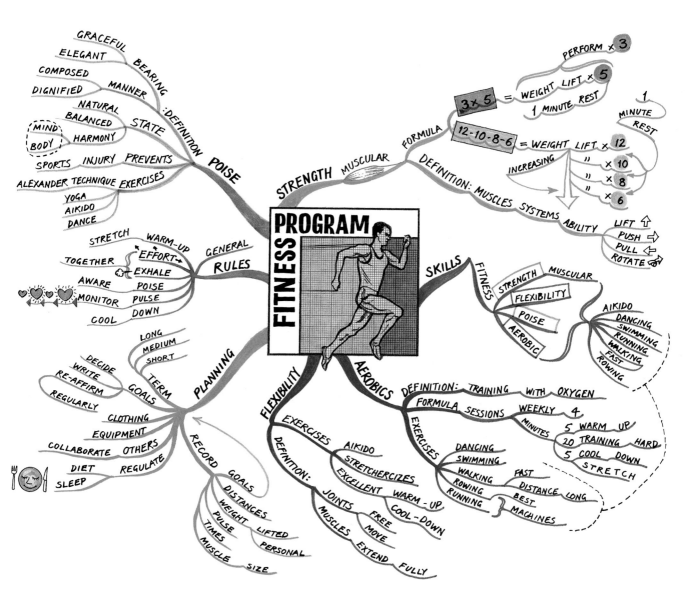

POISE

- DEFINITION:
  - MANNER
    - BEARING
      - GRACEFUL
      - ELEGANT
    - COMPOSED
    - DIGNIFIED
  - STATE
    - NATURAL
    - BALANCED
    - HARMONY
      - MIND
      - BODY
  - PREVENTS
    - INJURY
    - SPORTS
  - EXERCISES
    - ALEXANDER TECHNIQUE
    - YOGA
    - AIKIDO
    - DANCE

STRENGTH — MUSCULAR

- FORMULA
  - 3 × 5 = WEIGHT LIFT × 5
    - PERFORM × 3
    - 1 MINUTE REST
  - 12-10-8-6 = WEIGHT LIFT × 12
    - INCREASING
      - " × 10
      - " × 8
      - " × 6
    - 1 MINUTE REST
- DEFINITION: MUSCLES SYSTEMS ABILITY
  - LIFT
  - PUSH
  - PULL
  - ROTATE

RULES

- GENERAL
  - WARM-UP
    - STRETCH
    - EFFORT
      - TOGETHER
      - EXHALE
    - POISE
    - AWARE
  - COOL DOWN
    - MONITOR PULSE

PLANNING

- TERM
  - LONG
  - MEDIUM
  - SHORT
- GOALS
  - DECIDE
  - WRITE
  - RE-AFFIRM
  - REGULARLY
- REGULATE
  - CLOTHING
  - EQUIPMENT
  - OTHERS
    - COLLABORATE
  - DIET
  - SLEEP

RECORD

- GOALS
- DISTANCES
- WEIGHT LIFTED
- PULSE PERSONAL
- TIMES
- MUSCLE SIZE

FLEXIBILITY

- EXERCISES
  - AIKIDO
  - STRETCHERCIZES
  - EXCELLENT WARM-UP
  - COOL-DOWN
- DEFINITION:
  - JOINTS FREE MOVE
  - MUSCLES EXTEND FULLY

PROGRAM FITNESS

SKILLS

- FITNESS
  - STRENGTH MUSCULAR
  - FLEXIBILITY
  - POISE
  - AEROBIC
    - AIKIDO
    - DANCING
    - SWIMMING
    - RUNNING
    - WALKING FAST
    - ROWING

AEROBICS

- DEFINITION: TRAINING WITH OXYGEN
- FORMULA SESSIONS WEEKLY 4
  - MINUTES
    - 5 WARM UP
    - 20 TRAINING HARD
    - 5 COOL DOWN
    - STRETCH
- EXERCISES
  - DANCING
  - SWIMMING
  - WALKING FAST
  - ROWING DISTANCE LONG
  - RUNNING BEST MACHINES

Mind Map® 15

formulas, combined with **Big Bad Habits**, that we tend to become increasingly more rigid than is good for us.

When your body is flexible your muscles are able to extend to their full length, thus keeping them supple and avoiding the danger of damage to both them and your skeleton.

When your body is flexible your nervous system is also able to send its messages more smoothly to any part of your body without being pinched or blocked by areas of muscular rigidity and tension. Similarly oxygen can flow more freely through the joints, blood vessels and capillaries when your body is more open.

Flexibility is a deep-rooted and basic need. This is demonstrated in the stretch reflex – that frequent desire of ourselves and animals to have a good yawn or stretch (I've just automatically done so while writing this!). Stretching in all directions is one of the best flexibility exercises there is, and can be naturally and easily performed on a daily basis. One of the best instructors in this area of physical fitness is the cat! Other exercises that are specifically designed to increase flexibility include dance, yoga, gymnastics, the Japanese martial art of Aikido and aerobic "stretchercizes."

One of the best "quick and easy" stretching exercises is the "Salute to the Sun" developed in India. Yoga, which means "union", is especially good for developing flexibility in both body and mind! The Salute to the Sun can be performed in less than five minutes. In those five minutes you will have successfully stretched all the major muscle groups in your body. It consists of a sequence of positions that move the spine in various ways and promote flexibility in the limbs. It also regulates breathing and focuses the mind! (See illustrations opposite.)

Whenever you are doing any aerobic or strength training, your flexibility exercises should always be a major part of your warm-up and cool-down.

As you will now realize, it is essential throughout any stretching exercises that you maintain proper poise. Stretching off-balance can unnecessarily pull muscles, and tear ligaments and tendons. Before you begin any exercise, momentarily pause, compose yourself, make sure that your neck and joints are free, that your

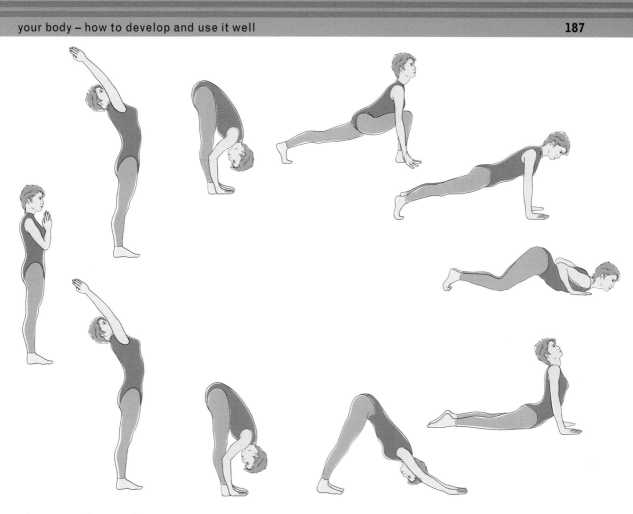

Figure 25: salute to the sun

head is balanced appropriately on your body, and that your back and torso are comfortably lengthened and widened.

4. strength

Muscular strength is an important part of your overall health. It refers to the ability of all your muscles and muscle systems to lift, pull, push and rotate.

Strength training has a number of advantages:

1. It tones up your muscles (remember, each one of your muscle fibers is a little "mini heart").
2. It strengthens your bones.
3. It allows greater general functional ability.
4. It gives you more power to perform any of the physical tasks in your everyday life.
5. It provides a solid basis for any sporting/athletic activity.
6. It lessens your chance of injury.
7. It helps protect your internal organs.
8. It increases self-confidence.
9. It brings you respect from others.
10. It makes you look good.
11. It makes you feel good!

There are also a number of myths surrounding strength and muscle-building exercises:

MYTH: "Muscles grow while you are working out."
TRUTH: Surprisingly, your muscles slightly *diminish* while you are working out. This is because, when weight-training properly (see page 191) you are wearing *down* your muscles by the effort you are producing. This extra strain on your muscles alerts your brain to mobilize its "repair and construction team" and to both fix the damage, and make that muscle even stronger and larger, in order to prepare it for what the body/brain predicts to be an immediate probability of further use.

In a sense, your body is being prepared, like a fine athlete, for the next "competition." And this happens *automatically*, *after* your exercise period. The energy for this will be pulled largely from your stored body fat, and will be used to "build you and bulk you up" during the time between your exercise bouts.

The ideal time for this "auto-training/construction" work is 48 hours. Thus weight-training for strength and muscle building is a 24-hour process! Therefore it is ideally done on average once every two days. (See page 196.)

MYTH: "It is known as 'weight-lifting' because *lifting* is what causes muscle growth."

TRUTH: The myth is only *half* true. It is weight-lifting *and* weight-lowering that stimulates muscle growth.

When you are lifting, your muscle is contracting. When you are lowering your muscle is lengthening. A good example of this is the bicep curl. When you are lifting the weight, you can actually see/feel the bicep contract, and thus bulge. When you lower the weight, you can see the bicep lengthen and the bulge disappear.

Both stages are just as important for the growth-of-the-muscle messages to be triggered by your brain, and your muscle must be challenged in *both* the contraction and the extension stage.

MYTH: "When women lift weights, they become chunkier and muscle-bound like men."

TRUTH: A woman's body responds to weight training and fitness exercises in the same way as a man's. Thus, depending on the heaviness of the weight and the number of repetitions (times it is lifted), the muscles can be made either more bulky or more lean. Whichever of these options is chosen, in the process, the percentage of fat will decrease.

When women exercise, the muscles they develop become firmer, but do not "bulge" in the same way that men's do. This is because their thicker layer of subcutaneous fat "smoothes out" the surface, allowing the body to retain its contours. Any exercises involving the lower back, stomach, hips and thighs, for example, actually slim these areas.

●   ●   ●

As you prepare for strength training exercises (and indeed for aerobic exercises as well) it is advisable to follow the *Head Strong* guidelines. These are designed to increase the probability that your training programme will be successful, to protect you from injury of any sort, and to make your entire fitness and health training more enjoyable.

- Decide what your overall health and fitness goals are.
- Write them down. The mere act of writing acts as a commitment, gives the **Good New Habit** an excellent start, and increases the probability that you will act by as much as 50 percent.
- Have a thorough check-up with your doctor/sports trainer/nutritionist in order to establish your current fitness and health levels. This will give you a good guide to the levels at which you should start.
- Regularly envision your goals. This will give you added boosters to the power of your **Good New Habit** and will increase your probability of success.
- Prepare yourself by selecting proper clothing and equipment (the best makes you feel and perform better). Make sure your workout conditions are as good as they can be, and that they support your goals.
- Where possible join forces with other people who are striving towards similar goals.
- Devise a short, medium and long-term fitness plan. Write this down and follow it, making appropriate adjustments where necessary.
- Keep records of your progress. This helps further develop the **Good New Habit**, gives you a reward for effort, and encourages you as you strive toward your vision.
- Make sure that your diet is designed to give you maximum support in your efforts.
- During the exercises, regularly repeat your favorite and most appropriate Brain Boosters. These again help build up the **Good New Habit** and also provide constant motivation. They act as your own personal internal super-coach.
- As a general rule, when exerting muscular effort, exhale.
- Constantly and encouragingly remind yourself, during all exercise, of appropriate poise and positioning. Hold images of excellent poise in your mind's eye as you perform your exercise routine.

- Always warm up thoroughly and stretch like a cat!
- Cool down thoroughly.
- Monitor your pulse and keep records of your "pulse-trends."
- Have fun!

the muscle building strength formula

Researchers from Tufts University did an experiment in which 86-96-year-old nursing home residents were engaged in an eight-week program of supervised weight training. The results showed that even with such a short time in training, the residents dramatically increased their strength and improved their balance in the process. Ongoing studies confirmed that weight training with either free weights or machines helped to restore lost bone density, diminished arthritic pains in the knee, and even moderated insulin insensitivity in type two diabetics.

As with aerobics, the formula for gaining muscle power is simple. Once again, the exercises need to be repeated four times weekly and can take between 20 and 60 minutes, depending upon the number of muscles and muscle groups you wish to strengthen.

Within the four-times weekly formula reside two other simple formulas for deriving maximum benefit from your weight training.

the 3 x 5 formulas

This means that you find a weight for the muscle group you are exercising that you can lift, push, pull or rotate a maximum of five times. After the fifth repetition you should be too exhausted to complete a sixth.

As an example, supposing that you are doing a simple lift (or "curl") for your biceps – the large muscles in your upper arm that enable you to lift things, and which are the muscles with which men traditionally show off their muscular power.

The *three x five* formula means that you repeat the exercise three times, and that in each set of these *three* times you lift the weight *five* times. In the first of these three sets, lift the weight five times, and then take a one-minute rest (which, if you have chosen the weights correctly, you *will* need!). During this rest the blood will flow to your freshly exercised muscles (aerobic fitness will help you here) and the muscles will be more "pumped up," ready for the second set of five lifts.

The second set should be performed in exactly the same manner, although it will probably be slightly easier than the first five lifts, because your muscles are now fully pumped up. Afterwards, rest for another minute to give your now well-worked muscles a chance to replenish their energy and recuperate.

The third set of five repetitions will be the most difficult, because your muscles will now be tired and stretched-to-the-limit from their previous efforts. The last lift of the last five should be one that pushes you to your limit, and which you can only j--u-u-u—s—t make.

During the third repetition of five lifts, your body will realize, as it did with your aerobic training, that its muscles are not really up to the task, and that too much effort is being required to perform the lifts. Its immediate response will be to increase the volume and strength of the muscle, and as such it will energetically build for you new muscle tissue during days of rest, thus building up the bulk, size and strength of the muscles you have exercised. When the weight becomes easier, which it will, simply add more weight, keeping to the *three x five* formula.

Higher numbers of repetitions, anywhere from 6 to 20, will progressively increase the *aerobic* fitness of the muscle and making it leaner and longer rather than bulky. Such exercising will provide less "power strength" and more "stamina strength."

the 12-10-8-6 formula

In this second of the two simple approaches you start with a lighter weight and perform 12 repetitions. This is a form of vigorous warm-up. After your minute's rest you increase the weight, and perform 10 repetitions. Again after a minute's rest, you increase the weight and perform eight repetitions. By this time your muscles will be beginning to feel a considerable stress. After another minute's rest the last set of six repetitions (or five if you wish) is exactly the same as the last set in your three x five formula.

Each of these approaches is extremely beneficial. Once you are "in" to your training routine, feel encouraged to experiment with the approach that serves you best.

The purpose of the final set in your weight exercises is to have you reach maximum effort - to be extended to full intensity. If you have worked out on an aerobic machine, you will know that the graphs of intensity start very low, and then build to a peak before trailing off. When you are at full intensity you are providing yourself with the maximum opportunity for producing positive change. The final set of repetitions is the weight-training equivalent of the Training Effect in aerobics. Without it, growth and change is much slower or does not take place.

At this point I want to emphasize to you that lifting that final set is, primarily, a *mental* exercise. You have to bring all your vision, commitment, dedication, focus and intensity to taking your body to that limit. Physical training is not simply "working on the body," you see. It is, vitally, working on and increasing the power of your mind.

Confirming yet again the *mens sana in corpore sano* principle, the greatest chess player of all time, Garry Kasparov, has publicly stated that one of the main reasons he becomes so physically fit and strong before a Grandmaster tournament is because it makes him feel stronger *in all senses* during his mental combat.

So what specific exercises should you do in order develop overall muscular strength?

The answer is surprisingly simple.

the *Head Strong* full-body strength workout

The muscle groups of your body are conveniently divided into only a few areas on which you need to work (see Figure 26):

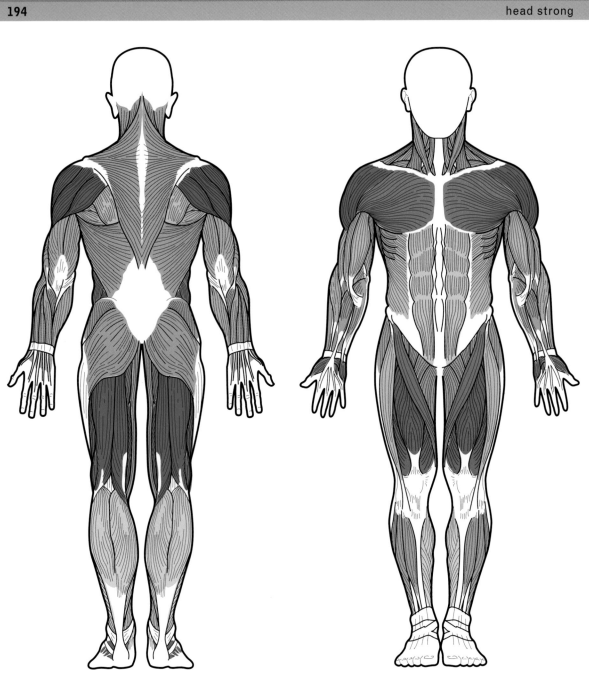

Figure 26: muscle groups

- Shoulders
- Chest
- Arms
- Back
- Torso (stomach)
- Legs

For a complete muscular workout you need to exercise each muscle group.

For your arms you need to develop the front (biceps) and back (triceps). For your legs you need to develop the front and back of the thigh (quadriceps and hamstrings) and the back of the lower leg (the calves).

And that's it!

For a complete body strength workout, you therefore need to do, fundamentally, only a "basic muscle pack" of exercises, using the minimum of equipment – either simple dumbbells or standard weight-training equipment, or just yourself!

Nine basic exercises, covering all the major muscle groups, are:

- Side raises with dumbbells for your shoulders
- Barbell bench presses, or push-ups for your chest
- Dumbbell "rows," performed half-kneeling with each arm in turn, for your back
- Bicep curls and tricep push-ups for your arms
- Dumbbell squats and lunges for your thighs (quadriceps and hamstrings)
- Angled calf-raises with dumbbells for your calves
- Floor crunches (sit-ups) for your abdominal muscles

Remember: *breathe out* when you are exerting yourself, and *breathe in* when you are relaxing. And the *three x five* formula – do the exercise five times in each set of three, resting for a minute between each repetition!

weight training and aerobics

As you will now understand, it is best to alternate your exercises – spending one day on weight training and body-building, and the next on aerobic exercises. This allows the Training Effects for both your heart muscles and your skeletal muscles to be maximized.

But, I hear you say, I don't have time for all of that! Are there exercises I can do that combine poise, aerobics, flexibility and strength?

Yes there are!

Head Strong's recommended super all-round exercises

swimming

Swimming is one of the best all-round exercises there is. It provides you with automatic aerobic training, helps to develop flexibility, and it encourages muscular development, especially when you do regular sprinting session in the pool – the equivalent of "Water Weight-Training!"

Swimming has the added advantage of being "non-impact" and therefore dramatically reduces the chance of physical stress-related injuries.

running

Running shares many of the advantages of swimming, in that it exercises all the muscles in your body, naturally incorporates aerobic training, and develops muscular strength as well. It is especially important in running to have excellent poise, as this massively decreases the chance of injury.

The advantage that running has over swimming is that you are "competing" with gravity; you therefore use more energy (you lose more calories!) per unit time.

This advantage is similarly a disadvantage, however, in that it involves your body in continuous impact with the ground.

Running will make you slimmer and leaner and "thinner," but if you want to incorporate muscle-building into your running program, include regular and consistent sprint training.

walking

To be a good all-round training exercise, walking needs to be fast! When it is, it becomes virtually identical to running - the main differences being that it uses slightly less energy per minute, and it involves far less impact on your joints, and therefore less chance of injury to ankles, knees and hips.

rowing

Rowing requires extreme aerobic fitness, and obviously at the same time demands that the body be flexible and extremely muscularly powerful. Poise is also a major factor, in that a well-balanced head significantly increases the pushing and pulling power of the athlete.

Rowing ergometers are now among the most popular general exercise machines, and are highly commended by *Head Strong*. One of their advantages is that they will give you a regular computer print-out of your efforts, which makes it extremely easy to keep a record of your progress. As with running and swimming, rowing exercises all of your main muscle groups and, like, swimming it is a non-impact exercise and therefore reduces your risk of injury during training.

dancing

Dancing, especially salsa, latin, free, jazz and classical is both a natural desire and one of the best all-round exercises there is, especially when you incorporate many different moves. Dancing encourages excellent poise, requires considerable muscular strength, especially in any lifting or throwing routines with partners, is one of the best methods of acquiring flexibility, and is similarly one of the best aerobic training sports when it is maintained at a high pace, non-stop, for periods of more than 20 minutes at a time.

It is also fun, making you happier, reducing your stress levels and involving and opening up your senses.

Whenever you have the social opportunity of doing a more static or sedentary activity or going to a club or dance, choose the dance!

the martial arts – aikido

This martial art, based on poise, balance, "reading" your attacker's body signals and language, and on sensory alertness, flexibility and maximum and efficient use of strength, has become one of the fastest growing physical and health-training movements in the world.

Its principles are completely in tune with the **Success Formula - TEFCAS** and **Meta-Positive Thinking**, and will give you a complete **Holanthropic** (body and mind) workout.

Aikido was developed by Morihi Ueshiba, in Japan. Nearly a century-and-a-half ago, as a young and weakly boy he watched in horror as his parents were beaten up by some local thugs. Powerless to do anything, and traumatized by the experience, he resolved to become the strongest man in Japan, and to then make the thugs pay for what they had done.

He stuck to his goal.

By the time he was a teenager Ueshiba was renowned as one of the strongest men in Japan. It was reported that if he could get his arms around the trunk of a tree, he would be able to uproot it.

Intrigued by the incredible effects his training had had on his body and health, Ueshiba began to study the martial art of Ju-Jitsu and Karate. Over a period of years he developed all his combined skills to become the strongest man in Japan, as well as the top martial artist. He established training schools, remained undefeated in combat, and was elevated to a "National Treasure of Japan," a privilege reserved for those who have contributed outstandingly to the mental and physical arts of the nation.

You would think this would be enough, but it wasn't!

By his late 50s, Ueshiba had realized that the martial arts at which he was an absolute master were gradually damaging him. Even when he won competitions, he would suffer injuries, the negative effects of which were tending to accumulate over time.

He thought there must be another way.

Ueshiba, tending more towards introspection and the investigation, like Matthias Alexander, of himself and his mental and physical processes, took his top martial arts students to a four-year retreat in order to find a "new way."

He succeeded. The new way became known as Aikido - "the Way of Harmony."

normal behavior – anti-olympian training

Now that you know how to acquire ultimate physical fitness, let's look at its opposite!

To gain a further and somewhat amusing perspective on the nature of developing and obtaining physical health, we will examine normal unhealthy behavior, from the Olympian point of view.

Imagine that you intend to go from nowhere on the physical scale to Olympian fitness - to the top. You hire a coach who is a little bizarre in his approach. He gives you the following rules for developing your body towards super fitness:

1. You must get up slightly late in order to add a certain "rushed edge" to your morning's routine.
2. For breakfast you must have a cup of coffee with milk and two spoons of sugar, accompanied by white bread covered with butter and jelly. This should be accompanied by at least one cigarette.
3. You must not walk, run, or cycle to work. You must drive every day.

4. Your job must be sedentary. For not more than two hours of your eight-hour day should you be out of a chair.

5. The air in your office must be air-conditioned and recirculated. It must not be fresh.

6. The light in your place of work should be incandescent, supplemented by as little natural light as possible.

7. Your lunch should consist of sandwiches or a quick bar lunch, accompanied by at least one alcoholic drink. Alternatively, you may have a quick deli snack.

8. Throughout your working day you should have at least eight cups of coffee, and if not, should substitute sweet soft drinks. These can be accompanied by chocolate bars, donuts or cookies.

9. At the end of your working day, you must again take the car. Once again you should not walk, run or cycle home.

10. As a break between work and home, you can, if you wish, visit a bar once again.

11. You are specifically encouraged not to do exercise of any sort in the evening.

12. Evening activities should include:
    - Having a drink when you get home.
    - Reading the newspaper.
    - Watching television.
    - Having a well-cooked three-course meal with adequate accompanying alcohol.

13. After dinner it is recommended that you do at least one extra hour of office work.

14. And so to bed!

In general you are encouraged to have as little exercise as possible. The exception to this is when you are instructed on an occasional (once every two to six weeks) basis to play violently active and strenuous games such as football or baseball.

If a coach were to try to force you into this kind of behavior under the guise of helping you to become more healthy and happy, you would throttle that coach! If you obeyed the coach, just imagine the consequences...

And yet for tens of millions of people around the world, what has been described above describes their normal day and their general lives.

Because this behavior becomes a **Big Bad Habit**, it becomes normal. This normalization process can have disastrous consequences, as in a macabre experiment with frogs. Frogs were placed in a large vat filled to the brim with water. Very, very gradually the temperature of the water was increased, the experimenters obviously expecting the frogs to jump out when the water became just too hot. To their surprise and amazement they did not! The frogs simply hung around in the water, behaving normally while becoming simultaneously more and more listless. As the heat continued to rise, the frogs gradually ceased all activity, eventually allowing themselves to be boiled to death.

It is similar with the insidious invasion of a wrong formula leading to a **Meta-Negative Thinking Habit**. Because the behavior appears "normal," and because the incremental changes are so tiny, the habit slinks in under the ramparts of consciousness, and the invaded and infected individual is sublimely and subliminally unaware.

To convince you even further of the need for physical fitness, let us look at the medical symptoms caused by *inactivity*:

1. The unused body deteriorates overall.
2. The lungs become weak and inefficient.
3. The heart muscle grows smaller and weaker.
4. The blood vessels become more clogged and more rigid.
5. The muscles lose strength, volume and tone.
6. Your systems for delivering energy throughout your body shrink and shrivel.
7. Overall body strength, functioning and power decline.

As a function of all the above, your immune system becomes weaker, and your vulnerability to illness and disease rises.

Stay Fit!

Studies of adults show that a sedentary lifestyle is as likely to cause heart disease as is high blood pressure, smoking or high cholesterol levels. People who fail to take physical exercise are thought to be twice as likely to contract coronary heart disease. They also run higher-than-average risks of developing breast cancer, diabetes and osteoporosis. In the U.S.A. alone, physical inactivity is estimated to cause 250,000 deaths per year.

New Scientist magazine, April 23, 1994

summary of general physical fitness

To be comprehensively fit you need to focus on the four pillars of Poise, Aerobic Fitness, Flexibility and Muscular Strength. The first three require specific exercises and routines, and are best worked into an overall exercise program.

When you are training, it is a useful idea to keep records. These should include, variously, time, distance covered, weight lifted, level reached, personal records broken, weight, muscle size, heart rate, etc. It is usually best to devise your own progress charts.

•   •   •

What, though, if you do everything you can, and get injured?

Perhaps my own story will shed some light on the appropriate approach.

During the early and particularly vigorous stages of my own physical and athletic career, like all other athletes I regularly suffered minor injuries.

These I found extremely frustrating, annoying and aggravating. I resented them!

When running, in particular, I would regularly sprain my left knee, and began to hate that part of my body for its constant interference with and interruptions of my "best laid plans." Then one day the universe sent me a flash of realization and inspiration.

I suddenly became aware that my knee, an incredible work of engineering genius, was one of my lifetime companions. It had been traveling with me from before the moment I was born, and had devoted its life, exclusively, willingly, and selflessly, to me and all my demands of it. Having supported (literally!) me and my activities and dreams for some 30 years, it was now trying to communicate with me in order to help.

It was saying something like: "Hey Tony! Help! ... I've been willingly helping you walk, run, swim, and dance for 30 years, and now your off-poise-balance is doing something that is hurting me! If you keep on this way, I won't be able to help you any more. Tony! ... I'm your friend! ... Please help me! I am trying to give you *Feedback* here ..."

From that moment on I looked upon all injuries and illnesses as communications from that vast army of friends and companions called my body and brain, whose sole purpose and pleasure in life was to please and support me. If they were any way in pain or dis-ease, then it was my responsibility and commitment to adjust the behavior that was causing them pain, and to care for them as they care for me.

If you take this more **Meta-Positive** approach, you will place your mind and body under considerably less stress.

To help you with this and to supplement your record keeping, complete the following Quick Brain-check.

quick brain-check 12 – chart yourself

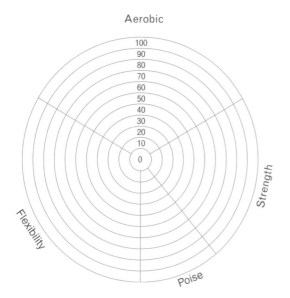

The circular graph opposite is designed to help you keep track of your improvements in your aerobic, flexibility and strength areas of physical fitness. In each area rate yourself on a scale of zero to 100, where zero means utterly unfit, and 100 means Olympic fitness level. Fill in the chart now, and then once every month as you progress with your training program.

summary

In order for you to develop the healthiest mind in the healthiest body, the following action steps are highly recommended:

1. Do aerobic training for at least 20 minutes, four times a week.
2. In conjunction with your aerobic training, increase your flexibility.
3. In conjunction with aerobics and flexibility, develop the strength of your entire muscular system.
4. Develop and improve your poise.
5. Create a mastermind group of health advisers as you would if you were a professional athlete (remember just how priceless your own body is). This group might include specialists, doctors, coaches, Alexander teachers and nutritional experts.

6. Incorporate regular rest periods in your daily, weekly, monthly, yearly and overall life – they will give that life more quality and help it be longer.

7. Find time to play. Play is one of the best forms of all round exercise, especially when you have the opportunity to play with children – they will make a hard workout in the gym appear like a rest period!

8. Establish and monitor a basic healthy diet (see Chapter 8).

9. Do a creative Mind Map® showing your current physical levels and your future goals. Immediately put these goals into action.

chapter eight

brain and body food

Through your thoughts and feelings you create your own well body.

Dr. Mike Samuels, Director, The Headlands Clinic, California

When you let your body receive the energies of the universe, when you are open to them and not closed, when you are relaxed and not tense, when you have positive ideas and not negative ideas, the energies of the universe will flow into your body to keep you well or to heal you. Your body's use for these energies is more powerful than any drug or herb, more powerful than any surgeon, and any healer known to man.

The Well Body Book, by Howell Bennett, Linda Bennett and Dr Mike Samuels

Having looked at how to keep your external body fit and in shape, in this chapter we will see how we can look after a human from the *inside* – how good nutrition and diet are crucial for the health and well-being of your body and mind.

the immortal machine

One day when I was in my mid-twenties, and had suffered a series of minor injuries and colds, I went to my doctor in whinging mood. Not realizing then that my injuries had been caused by misuse, and my minor illnesses by anti-body behavior, I began to complain about how non-functional and weak the body was in comparison to the brain.

Like a good but momentarily angry teacher, my doctor turned on me, and in a few minutes had set the record straight and permanently transformed my body-thinking.

He said something that truly astonished me. He said that in all his years as a doctor, dealing with the incredible number of diseases and injuries of his thousands of patients, one thing, and one thing only had impressed him. Not the weakness of the body, but its incredible, virtually indomitable, strength. The doctor went on to explain that there was also one and only one question which still perplexed him. He could not understand, with his intimate knowledge of the complexity and miraculous nature of the human being, why any of us ever died!

your three-million-year old healer

Dr. Mike Samuels and Hal Bennet are in the same camp as my own doctor. They consider the human body to be a learning, surviving and healing mechanism that has spent three million years practicing the **Success Formula – TEFCAS**, to produce a mind-boggling work of medical mastery! (If you believe in evolution, you can extend this even further, to include a four billion-year **Success Formula** experiment by the Universe to produce *you*.)

As you read on, I am sure you will increasingly agree with them.

Take a quick look back to Chapter 7, pages 148–9, and see the astonishing catalogue of what your body is actually composed. Next consider what those 60 trillion body cells of yours, and especially the 22 trillion blood cells, do for you.

Each one of your cells is an independent and interdependent unit of life and intelligence. To keep you alive they join together in an army trillions of times bigger than all the combined armies that have ever existed on Earth.

This incomparable army subdivides itself into many units, including:

- Supporters – your bones.
- Universe-analyzers, look-outs and early-warning systems – your billion-faceted senses.
- Manufacturers – the trillions of cells devoted to every aspect of your growth and to your energy supplies.
- Carriers – these subdivide into those cells which take away waste and those which deliver nutrients to and from every cell of your body – the distances they cover are billions of times longer than their own size. Their accomplishments make even those of the pyramid builders look minuscule!
- General helpers – these vast armies store, process, maintain and regulate.
- Fighters – these are your antibodies, composed mainly of protein. They fight millions of battles on thousands of fronts every day of your life. Their ratio of victories to defeats is in the 99.9+ percent success range! Their equipment and methods of combat make black-belt martial artists and Star Wars technology look primitive!

We often marvel at the industry, complexity and immaculate organization of the ants' nest. The miraculous body, which is working for you even as you read these words, is a million million-times more complex! And all of these processes and tasks undertaken by your army of cells happen without your "conscious brain" (your cerebral cortex) being involved.

Does this vast army need your help?

Indeed it does!

First it needs you to make sure that you are *aerobically* fit. When you are, each of your 22 trillion blood cells is individually fitter and stronger and more able to carry out vital tasks. Their immediate commander, your heart, is also bigger, more powerful, more relaxed and resilient under pressure, and more indefatigable.

Secondly you need to be *poised* and *flexible* in order to allow the entire communication system to operate fluently, and to keep the pathways through which the armies travel open and free of obstruction.

Thirdly you need your muscles to be fit and *strong*, in order that your billions of mini-hearts can give their full support.

The above underlines even more emphatically the need for physical fitness outlined in the previous chapter.

Is there more you can do to support your extraordinary body-forces?

Yes there is – a lot! In addition to general body *fitness*, you need general body *health*.

Your body needs a superb diet, freedom from negative stress, the right mental attitude, balanced sleep and rest, freedom from the inappropriate and over use of drugs, and good helpings of love and affection! If you interfere with any of these natural functions, you literally disable your army. You put every single one of your cells *not* at ease; *ill* at ease; *dis*-eased.

You will realize from this that your brain, mind and spirit work in absolute integration with your incredible body, the brain of which is its prime organ.

Increasingly you will see why the motto of Holanthropy is: *mens sana in corpore sano* – a healthy mind in a healthy body. The rest of this chapter and the next are devoted to helping you help your brain and mind help your body.

feeding your body and mind

A United States survey of more than 107,000 men and women in 49 states was conducted by researchers from the National Center for Chronic Disease Prevention and Health Promotion in the mid-1990s.

The study concluded that most of the people had no idea of how to eat a healthy diet, little idea of how to exercise, and virtually no idea of the beneficial relationship of proper diet and good exercise:

- 35 percent of men and 40 percent of women who said they were trying to lose weight were not aware of the number of calories they were consuming, or of the nutritional content of their diet.
- Of those who *were* exercising, 58 percent of the men and 63 percent of the women were exercising, in total, less than 150 minutes per week.
- Knowledge of the relationship between nutrition and exercise was minimal.

These findings were even more surprising, given the fact that Americans spend US$33 billion every year on weight-loss products and services, most of which is apparently wasted.

In pursuit of the ideal healthy diet, two questions arise. First, what have the human tribes throughout the ages used as their main diet? Second, what, basically, are we as human beings *designed* to eat?

the hunter gatherers

The average human tribe, for the bulk of the 3 million years or so that hominoids have lived on the planet, did not cultivate its own food. Their numbers were so small and the supplies of food in general so large that farming was unnecessary.

It seems that the vast majority of them were "omnivores" – they ate virtually *anything* that was edible and available.

Their diets were therefore mainly seasonal, and consisted of greens, roots, seeds and nuts, berries and fruits, insects, eggs, and occasionally, when they could catch them, birds and small animals. Those who lived by lakes, rivers and seas (which again was the vast majority), had a diet richly supplemented with a wide variety of crustaceans and fish, and often the various forms of seaweed.

By 3 million-year old habit, then, and by environmental prerogative, the diet of the human being has been one rich in vegetables, nuts and fruits, supplemented by fish and animal fat and protein. In addition to the contents of their diet, we also know that most of the food our ancestors ate was fresh and usually mature, or ripe.

what are we designed to eat?

Our next question is what we are designed to eat? The simplest way to answer this is to look at our digestive system, starting with the teeth and mouth, traveling down to the stomach, and visiting our small and large intestines.

We can get a pretty good feel for the purpose of our own design by looking at the animals representing the two extremes of eating – the carnivores and the herbivores. The carnivores, typified by the big cats, have giant, elongated ripping teeth, very few chewing teeth, and a stomach and intestinal system specifically designed to ingest meat. In contrast, herbivores, typified by cows and sheep, have sharp, flat, cutting and pulling front teeth, no elongated teeth, a massive array of grinders, and a digestive system specifically designed to ingest leaves and grass.

What about us?

Our teeth indicate that we are more on the herbivore side of things. We do, however, have ripping teeth, and a digestive system designed to digest almost anything! We are, by design, as we are by 3 million-year-old habit, that wonderfully freeing concept and word: *omnivores*.

body and brain food

Having found that we are designed to eat almost everything and anything, let's look first at a few popular myths which, as soon as they are dispelled, will rapidly improve your health.

MYTH: Your body needs salt. Therefore use liberal doses of table salt in your cooking and on your meat and veg.

TRUTH: Your body *does* need salt. However, a good and well-rounded diet will provide most of this. Your average daily salt need is 1,000 milligrams (about half a small teaspoon) a day. This should be the *maximum* you use, as processed foods (which should be eaten very sparingly in a healthy diet) are riddled with salt. Just check the labels on the cans...

According to the January 2001 issue of the New England Journal of Medicine, most people overdose massively on salt, considerably raising their blood pressure, especially for those with hypertension – a silent condition which increases the risk of both strokes and heart-attacks. The study found that heavy salt users who reduced their intake to around 1,000 milligrams a day lowered their blood pressure – even those with previously normal blood pressure – regardless of race or gender.

MYTH: Sugar boosts your energy levels, and therefore should be taken before any physical or mental activity.

TRUTH: You need sugar. *Natural* sugar. This means sugar contained in fruits and vegetables, which also contain the vitamins and minerals needed for your body to metabolize the sugar. Refined sugar does not contain the nutrients required for its own metabolism, and in order to be used, your body has to rob itself by consuming its own supply of B vitamins. Eating refined sugars gives you a momentary energy boost, which is then followed by a loss of energy greater than that which the sugar gave you. This is why heavy sugar eaters often feel lethargic and depressed a short while after bingeing, and why long-distance athletes who take sugar before their event feel hyped-up for a moment, and then collapse.

MYTH: Eating well means having three square meals a day.
TRUTH: "Eating well" means something slightly different! The bear and other hibernating animals are designed to "binge" eat - store up massive reserves of fat which will supply energy through the sleeping months. These animals stuff themselves in giant one-off feasts and orgies. We humans are more like the vegetarian grazing animals such as sheep and cows. And when do they eat? Almost constantly!

For us, it seems that an ideal pattern is to eat more regularly and lightly throughout the day, perhaps consuming four to six smaller and lighter meals during the day, one every few hours.

If you eat in this way, you will tend to burn slightly more calories, will not have that stuffed and lethargic feeling you experience after a "square meal," and will therefore be more "light" throughout the day. Eating smaller meals will also give your digestive system less arduous work, and will allow the smaller food portions to be more effectively and efficiently absorbed and processed by you.

Another important by-product of such a habit of eating is that your body and brain will be being given the subliminal messages that "there's plenty of food out there!" This being the case, there will be no survival-desire to "stock up" in case the supply runs out.

MYTH: Eating well means having a big breakfast.
TRUTH: Yes AND No. Dr. Andrew Strigner, FRSM, former President of the McCarrison Society which investigates the medical effects of nutrition on health, has an amusing and cogent perspective.

Dr. Strigner points out that it is useful to look at the origin of meals such as the "traditional English breakfast" of eggs, sausages, bacon, beans, tomatoes, mushrooms, and fried bread.

From whence did this originate?

From English farmers.

And when did they eat this big breakfast?

After two hours of hard labour between 5:00 a.m. and 7:00 a.m., in the cold English dawn, during which time they lifted, carried, climbed, dug and milked!

They had done the equivalent of a two-hour intense aerobic and strength workout! They *needed* a big breakfast! If you have chosen, sensibly, to do your physical training in the morning, then by all means have a big breakfast. But if you are among the majority who slide out of bed and within half-an-hour are having your breakfast, have a light breakfast to "get you started," and eat lighter meals throughout the day.

MYTH: Fat is bad for You. Fat is cited as the cause of diabetes, clogged arteries, heart-attacks, the raising of cholesterol levels, as well as your blood-pressure. It is also reported to increase the amount of uric acid in your system, which contributes to the development of gout, arterial sclerosis and arthritis. In addition to all these heinous crimes, fat is known to play a significant role in degenerative diseases and premature aging. Excess fat also predisposes you to arterioscleroses, strokes, bladder disease and cancer. In summary, fat increases the risk of disability or death in almost all diseases. On top of all this it slows you down, makes movement uncomfortable or in some cases impossible, makes you feel bad, and looks gross!

TRUTH: *Excess* fat is bad for you. Fat is in fact not only good for you, it is so essential that without it you would die! The above statements are in fact only half truths. It is not *fat* to which they refer. It is to *excess* fat.

Now for the *good* news.

Research by Simon Coppack at the Royal London Medical School, and Steve O'Rahilly, an adipose tissue expert from the University of Cambridge, have revealed that fat sits at the heart of a complex and wide-ranging communications network. The revolutionary discovery they have made is that your fat is a giant *organ*! Not only an organ, but now recognized as one of the largest organs of your body. Their discoveries *"made fat much cleverer than it was thought to be before,"* says O'Rahilly.

What, then, have we recently discovered that your fat does for you?

Fat, unlike your other organs, is spread throughout your body in a number of specialised depots. It is packed around all your internal organs to protect them from trauma. It insulates and keeps you warm; cushions your joints, and increases their ability to repair and maintain themselves. It reduces inflammation, and is an essential part of your haemoglobin (oxygen-carrying red blood cells), allowing them to easily glide into capillaries, thus giving you a better supply of oxygen and nutrients to your tissues, and thereby increasing energy.

Fat stores and dynamically "doles out" appropriate portions of fat/energy in times of need. It supports testosterone levels which, among other things, influence and improve muscle strength and metabolism. Fat actively manufactures the hormone called leptin, which briefs your brain on the state of your body's energy coffers. Finally, fat, with water, is the main constituent of the very brain it advises and helps build.

The right sort of fat is *essential*!

food for thought

Eat with intelligence and become more intelligent!

A study at the Institute of Food Research in Reading, England, in 1999, found that women who dieted in order to get thin (negative thinking disguised as positive thinking – see Chapter 4, pages 72–3) didn't just lose pounds, but also memory power, reaction time and attention span.

The study, on 69 female volunteers, found that it was not the diet itself, but the stress associated with this growing **Big Bad Habit**, that caused the decline in mental performance. *The Times* newspaper summarized it pithily in an editorial on September 17th, 1999:

Women who try to get thin end up rather thick. Ask dieters a question and they will have a fat chance of answering it ... the more they fast the slower they become ... food dictates mood. And less means stress."

mood and memory

Dr. David Benson, of the University of Wales, Swansea tested 832 young women on their ability to remember a list of words. The results were intriguing: those who failed to eat breakfast had gloomy moods and poor memories; those who ate breakfast were happier, more positive, and had much better memories. Dr. Benson suggested that the increased blood-glucose levels of the breakfast-eaters were responsible for their superior performance.

nutritional effects

Dr. Michael Colgan, at the Nutritional Institute at the University of Auckland, directed three seminal studies on the effects of nutrition on aerobic stamina, strength, and IQ and behavior.

diet and stamina

In the first study four experienced male marathon runners, aged 26 to 35, were split into pairs, matched for age, marathon experience, previous marathon times and stage of training. Their mineral and vitamin levels were also factored in.

For six months, the first pair were given vitamin and mineral supplements to provide them with maximum nutritional health. The other two were given placebos that looked and tasted like the real supplements, but contained no vitamins or minerals.

All the athletes believed they had been receiving real supplements.

To make the experiment more interesting, after three months, again without their knowledge, the group that had been receiving real supplements was given placebos, and vice versa.

The results were dramatic. The runners who had been on supplements for the first three months showed dramatic improvement during that time. When taken off the supplements their performances declined. On the other hand, the runners who had been on placebos for the first three months showed a very slight improvement during that time. When they went on the real supplements for the final three months, their performances rocketed. One runner who had improved his initial marathon time by two minutes and eight seconds in the three months with placebos, improved, with proper nutrition, a further eight minutes and fifty-two seconds!

diet and strength

In the second study, the procedure was identical to that of the aerobic study, this time testing the athletes on one-arm curls, and some of the Olympic weightlifts.

In the first three months, the placebo weightlifters improved their performances between 10 and 20 percent; the nutritionally complete lifters improved their performances by between 40 and 60 percent!

During the second three months, those who had been deprived of complete nutrition showed an actual decline in performance, whereas those who were on full nutrition improved their performance by three times over what they had done in the first three months.

diet and IQ

The third study was undertaken at the University of Auckland Psychology Clinic and involved 16 cases of children classified as minimally brain-damaged, hyperactive or slow learners. In all cases, their diets were adjusted to reduce the levels of toxic metals in their bodies, eliminate allergies, and to diminish the amount of processed foods, soft drinks and sweets they ate.

As Dr. Colgan reported: "Over periods from three to six months, every case showed improvements in behaviour, at home, at school and in the clinic, as well as in motor co-ordination, speech articulation and reading skills."

What Dr. Colgan did not expect was perhaps the most significant finding of the study. "We found improvements between *five and thirty-five IQ points*, with an average improvement of 17.9 points ... we were convinced ... nutritional changes were the significant variable. They were making the children more intelligent and more emotionally stable."

fatheads!

A study at the Canadian Baycrest Center for Geriatric Care in Toronto focused on the mental effects of a fat-rich diet. Two groups of one-month old rats were fed on a diet that was nutritionally complete. The only difference between the groups was that the control group had only 10 percent of their calories come from fat. The experimental group had 40 percent of their calories from fat.

At four months of age, the equivalent of late adolescence in human beings, the rats were given a learning and memory task.

The low-fat diet rats fared well. However, the high-fat diet rats performed much more poorly. "High-fat diets impair performance on virtually all our measures," said Gordon Winocur, one of the leaders of the study. "It's remarkable how impaired these animals are."

The researchers reckoned that fat prevents the brain taking up glucose, possibly by interfering with the action of insulin, which helps regulate blood-sugar levels. High-fat diets often cause insulin resistance. People with signs of adult-onset diabetes, often caused by obesity, are also known to have memory problems.

So how do you incorporate fat *healthily* into your diet? More on that shortly. First, though, let's look at that which is most often associated with fat – calories.

calories

We have an obsession with calories! Yet many people haven't the faintest idea what a calorie is! A calorie is simply a measure of energy. It is the energy needed to raise the temperature of one gram of water through one degree centigrade.

This gives us some very important data: first that a calorie is a quite small amount of energy; secondly, that it will be possible and even easy to measure our calorific intake and output; and thirdly, that our bodies are incredibly efficient at converting matter into energy.

The statistics on the number of calories we need for survival are fascinating:

1. For *minimum* maintenance, which means keeping your heart and cardiovascular system functioning, breathing, digesting and maintaining temperature, and doing nothing else, you need *1,500 calories per day*.

2. To drift out of bed, drive to work in a car, take the elevator upstairs, sit at your desk for most of the day, drive back home, and spend most of the evening watching television before going to bed, you need, in addition to your basic 1,500 calories, another 800, giving a total of *2,300 calories per day*. (It should be mentioned that this is very, and deterioratingly! unfit.)

3. To maintain very minimal fitness, which will involve walking, minimally lifting, and being very gently active for at least two hours a day, you need only an extra 300 calories. This gives you a daily consumption of *2,600 calories*.

4. To maintain a *very fit* exercise regime five days per week, you need an extra 500 calories per day, giving you a daily consumption of 3,100 calories.

Now you know how many calories your body needs, how much do you need to exercise in order to maintain whatever level of health you personally wish? The table below will give you some idea of calorie expenditure.

activity time needed to consume 100 calories

minutes	activity
7	Run 1,500 yards (7.3 mph)
9	Bicycle 2 miles (13 mph)
9	Swim 400 yards (45 ypm)
10	Downhill skiing
14	Tennis
20	Golf
20	Gardening
20	Walk 1,500 yards (2.6 mph)
22	Bowling
31	Washing, showering, shaving, etc.
80	Reclining in bed

calorie healing power

A 10-year study of 17,000 men between the ages of 35 and 74, cited by health expert Leslie Kenton, showed the power of calorie-use to keep you well. Through all age ranges, those who expended fewer than 2,000 calories per week in exercise were *64 percent* more likely to suffer a heart-attack than those who exercised above the 2,000 calorie barrier.

The point about calories is that if you eat more calories than you use up in activities on a daily basis, the excess calories tend to accumulate, and you put on weight. Many illnesses and diseases are either caused or exacerbated by being overweight, and if you want to improve your health, one of the best ways to start is to find out what your ideal weight should be, and stick to it!

A point to bear in mind is that weight is only one factor in your overall health picture. Two people can be of the same height and weight, yet vary vastly in their overall health and fitness.

When you start your programme of overall physical fitness and strength training, you may notice, surprisingly, only slight losses in weight. Do not be discouraged! Something good is happening...

As you exercise, you *will* burn off fat; you will also *create* and *grow* extra muscle mass. This will be especially true in the first two to six months of your training. During this time you may be roughly maintaining *weight*; but you will be profoundly altering *shape*. Once your initial muscle-building has taken place, the reduction of weight on the scale will reflect, accurately, weight loss.

And there is more good news.

At this stage of your training, when the scales say you are losing a pound a week, you are losing a lot more than a pound of fat! For at the same time, in addition to the slight gain in muscle weight that will continue to accrue, you will be increasing the size and quantity of your entire cardiovascular system and the blood within it. The blood vessels you already have will become bigger and stronger, in addition to which you will add many miles of new capillaries. This is *good* weight gain, and represents healthy and beneficial weight loss/gain/adjustments. (For more on this see Chapter 7.)

●   ●   ●

The three main sources of our energy are fats, carbohydrates and proteins.

the "big three" – fats, proteins and carbohydrates
good fats, bad fats

You already know that fat is one of your largest organs, is a major provider and protector, is an essential source of your energy, and *needs* its stores regularly replenished. For this, you need not just "any old" fat; you need what are known as the Omega-3 fatty acids.

The Omega-3 fatty acids are commonly found in flax seed oil and fish oils. These healthy fats contain substances that every cell in your body requires to function, and therefore should be included in a good diet. The Omega-3s both reduce the risk of blood clots forming in your arteries, and lower the amount of triglycerides, another "bad" fatty substance in your blood.

The "good fats" are increasingly being classified as "essential nutrients," and are now known to be especially helpful in the building of muscle. Dr. Udo Erasmus, one of the world's leading experts on fat and nutrition says, "Essential fats increase the joints' ability to repair and maintain themselves, and also have an anti-inflammatory effect."

Erasmus goes on to say, in the context of physical training:

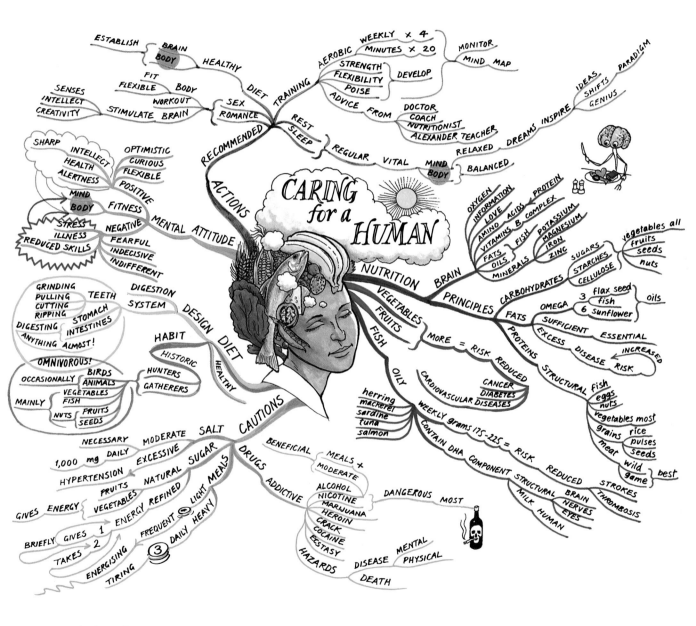

ESTABLISH · BRAIN · BODY · HEALTHY · DIET

FIT · FLEXIBLE · BODY

SENSES · INTELLECT · CREATIVITY · STIMULATE BRAIN · WORKOUT

SEX · ROMANCE

TRAINING · AEROBIC · WEEKLY × 4 · MINUTES × 20 · MONITOR · MIND MAP

STRENGTH · FLEXIBILITY · POISE · DEVELOP

ADVICE FROM · DOCTOR · COACH · NUTRITIONIST · ALEXANDER TEACHER

REST · SLEEP · REGULAR · VITAL · MIND · BODY · RELAXED · BALANCED

DREAMS INSPIRE · IDEAS · SHIFTS · PARADIGM · GENIUS

RECOMMENDED ACTIONS

SHARP · INTELLECT · HEALTH · ALERTNESS · OPTIMISTIC · CURIOUS · FLEXIBLE · POSITIVE

MIND · BODY · FITNESS

STRESS · ILLNESS · REDUCED SKILLS · NEGATIVE · FEARFUL · INDECISIVE · INDIFFERENT

MENTAL ATTITUDE

CARING for a HUMAN

NUTRITION

OXYGEN · INFORMATION · LOVE · AMINO ACIDS · PROTEIN · VITAMINS · B COMPLEX · FATS · FISH · POTASSIUM · MAGNESIUM · IRON · ZINC · OILS · MINERALS

BRAIN · PRINCIPLES

CARBOHYDRATES · SUGARS · STARCHES · CELLULOSE

vegetables all · fruits · seeds · nuts

FATS · OMEGA · 3 · flax seed · fish · 6 · sunflower · oils

SUFFICIENT · ESSENTIAL · EXCESS · DISEASE · INCREASED RISK

PROTEINS · STRUCTURAL · fish · eggs · nuts · vegetables most · grains · rice · pulses · seeds · meat · wild game · best · STROKES · THROMBOSIS

GRINDING · PULLING · CUTTING · RIPPING · TEETH · DIGESTION · SYSTEM

STOMACH · INTESTINES · DIGESTING · ANYTHING ALMOST!

DESIGN DIET

HABIT · HISTORIC · HUNTERS · GATHERERS · HEALTHY

OMNIVOROUS! · OCCASIONALLY · BIRDS · ANIMALS · VEGETABLES · MAINLY · FISH · NUTS · FRUITS · SEEDS

VEGETABLES · FRUITS · FISH · OILY

MORE = RISK REDUCED

herring · mackerel · sardine · tuna · salmon

CARDIOVASCULAR DISEASES · CANCER · DIABETES

WEEKLY grams 175–225 = RISK REDUCED

CONTAIN DHA COMPONENT STRUCTURAL · BRAIN · NERVES · EYES · MILK HUMAN · REDUCED

CAUTIONS

NECESSARY · MODERATE · SALT

1,000 mg DAILY · EXCESSIVE · HYPERTENSION · SUGAR · NATURAL · FRUITS · VEGETABLES · REFINED · DRUGS

GIVES ENERGY · BRIEFLY · GIVES · 1 · ENERGY · FREQUENT · LIGHT MEALS · TAKES · 2 · ENERGISING · 3 · DAILY HEAVY · TIRING · MEALS

BENEFICIAL · MEALS + MODERATE · ALCOHOL

ADDICTIVE · NICOTINE · MARIJUANA · HEROIN · CRACK · COCAINE · ESTASY

DANGEROUS · MOST

HAZARDS · DISEASE · MENTAL · PHYSICAL · DEATH

Mind Map® 16

A natural oil blend of flax seed [Omega-3] and sunflower oil [Omega-6 – another "good" fat] is a must for body-builders who want to add strength, because the essential fats are used up with training and have to be replenished. I suggest that body-builders use, daily, one teaspoon of oil for every 15 pounds of body weight. Oils can be added to cold and warm foods, but never to bake or fry – the high heat destroys them.

The "bad" fats are those found in chicken and turkey skin, sausages, hamburgers, marbled meats, whole-milk dairy products, margarine, biscuits, cakes and fried foods. These are the fats which your body finds it difficult to transform, and which can clog your system.

The "good" fats, especially those found in the popular fish salmon, trout, tuna, mackerel and herring, are also known as HDLs (high-density lipoproteins). Raw garlic also raises the level of HDL in your blood, and so does exercise:

There is a wealth of evidence linking exercise to raised HDL levels. One study in women showed that running improved HDL, and that the greater the level of exercise, the higher HDL level rose.

Dr. John Briffa, Medical Consultant to *Good Health*, *Daily Mail*

Confirming the value of "good" fat was the study reported in December 2000 in the Journal of the American Geriatrics Society. This confirmed that the "good fat" burns off the "bad" fat that causes such diseases as arterial sclerosis, and increases the length of life.

the power of protein

The second major source of energy is *protein*. Protein is a nitrogen-based organic compound that is used to build most of the structural components of your body and its tissues. It is an essential part of your diet.

Protein can be found in all fish and all meat; eggs; whole grains, including rice; pulses; beans; seeds; nuts; and in small quantities in most vegetables.

carbohydrates

Carbohydrates are a large group of compounds, which contain those elements vital for your survival – carbon and hydrogen. They include sugars; starches, such as potatoes; and all vegetables, seeds, nuts and fruits. They are not present at all in eggs, fish or meats.

Ideally your carbohydrates should be eaten in as natural a state as possible, and as fresh as possible. The more they have been refined, the more they will have been deprived of their natural ingredients – the vitamins, fiber, minerals and other essential energy sources that are vital to your own health. A diet based on naturally grown and fresh carbohydrates is powerfully health-enhancing, and has been found to protect against degenerative diseases such as arterial sclerosis, arthritis and cancer.

As well as being good "body food," carbohydrate grains such as wheat, rice, oats, corn, rye and buckwheat are also good "brain food." They enhance the production of serotonin, an important neurotransmitter that helps and enhances your mental and thinking functioning and skills.

vitamins

One other vital part ingredient of a healthy diet are vitamins. Vitamins are life-givers and life-sustainers. They are essential for normal growth and nutrition, and protecting and strengthening your immune system. What distinguishes them is that they are required in only small quantities in your diet, and unlike many other products, they cannot be made (synthesized) by your body. You have to acquire them from external nutrition.

Vitamins are present mainly in fruit and vegetables, but can also be found in eggs, liver and grains and fish. A good, balanced diet should provide you with all the vitamins you need, but they may need a boost with a good multi-vitamin supplement if you are run-down or unwell.

you are what you eat!

Does the quality of the food you eat make a difference to your physical health and, most importantly, your brain-power? Yes it does, and there is increasing evidence supporting the case! A diet that will keep your mind and body healthy needs to consist of foods that have specific value for the heart and cardiovascular system, the digestive system, the brain and the nervous system. Through the centuries, certain dietary principles have been discovered that are constant and common to all healthy eating and physical disciplines.

general principles

Eat fresh-picked food wherever possible. Fresh food has the advantage of being "complete" and containing more vitamins, minerals and nutrients than food that has been stored or tinned.

Eat a diet rich in variety. A varied diet allows your body to select from a wider range of possibilities those things it particularly needs at any moment in time. Eating the same foods regularly, or the same foods on certain given days, gives rise to the probability of over-providing the system with certain nutrients, or depleting some necessary element.

Look at yourself. On a regular basis stand naked, both front on and side on, in front of a mirror. Look at yourself objectively, and decide whether you look as healthy and fit as you should. If not, take appropriate dietary and other action; if you are satisfied with your appearance, continue the good practice! Start a **Good New Habit**. *"Listen" to yourself.* Much of your eating behavior is simply habit. We often say "yes" to every proffered snack or tit-bit, "yes" to every possible cup of tea or coffee, and "yes" to ourselves when looking at an item on the menu that we "know we like." When choosing food, especially in company, imagine that you are on your own, and go for food and drink which you would actually choose if you had the widest choice available and were eating what you really felt like.

When two-year-old children were placed in a room with every possible food available, the experimenters became most concerned on the first day when one little boy stuffed himself with chocolates, and another chose to eat 10 bananas. By the end of two weeks, however, every child had selected for him or herself a totally balanced diet. Let your body use its natural intelligences to select what it needs.

The following recommendations constitute a good basic diet for both your body and brain. Variations on these themes are an entirely personal matter, and should be explored with consideration and care for the ultimate benefit of your body.

vegetables and fruit

Vegetables should form the base of any healthy diet. They are rich in nutrients, and contain ample fiber for cleansing the digestive tract and keeping it muscularly fit and flexible. They are quickly and easily digested, and can, if eaten sensibly, form a complete diet in themselves. Similarly, fruit should be included in a balanced diet.

Gladys Block of the University of California at Berkeley, recently published a major review of more than 200 nutritional studies. The results were crystal clear: those who regularly ate substantially more vegetables and fruit than average were up to four times less likely to succumb to a huge range of cancers, including those of the breast, lung and colon. They were also less likely to suffer from heart disease.

In a different study over a 10-year period, vegetarians were found to be 24 percent less likely than non-vegetarians to die of ischemic heart disease, including heart-attacks.

nuts, seeds and whole grains

These are all highly concentrated sources of "brain food." Incidentally, since they contain all the genetic information necessary for plant life, they may in a sense be considered to be the brains of plants.

fish

Fish has traditionally been considered *the* "brain food," and research by Professor Michael Crawford, Director of the Institute for Brain Chemistry and Human Nutrition, has confirmed this assumption. Around 60 percent of the brain is built from specialized fats (the lipids) or liquids, most of which we cannot manufacture in our own systems but have to take in from the food chain. The primary source of these essential fats is fish. Crawford goes so far as to posit the theory that the development of human intelligence and genius is largely due to the development of societies around lakes, river-basins and coastlines, where there was an abundant supply of this essential brain food.

In a study entitled "Children of the Nineties," scientists at the University of Bristol, England, asked 435 pregnant women to keep a detailed diary of what they ate throughout their pregnancy. Three years later the team tested how well their children could recognize depth in three-dimensional images – one of the main measures for brain development.

The findings were significant: children of mothers who ate oily fish at least once a fortnight during pregnancy had by far the best scores. "Children of mothers who ate fish were one-and-a-half times as likely to have adult-grade 3-D vision as children whose mothers hadn't eaten any fish," said one of the scientists, Cathy Williams. The "magic ingredient," suggests Williams, "is the fatty acid DHA found in oily fish. This acid is a major structural component of brain, nerve and eye tissue and plays a vital role in the early development and continued development of these organs. It is interesting to note that it is abundant in human breast milk."

Further support for fish in the diet comes from the a study reported in January 2001 in the journal of the American Medical Association. The study concluded that women who consume as little as 225 grams of fish per week cut their risk of suffering a stroke by as much as half.

meat

Meat can be highly nutritious, and should be eaten by those who choose to two or three times a week maximum. The danger with many meats is that they can be suffused with synthetic chemicals, and so it is better to eat organic meat, or wild meat and game where possible.

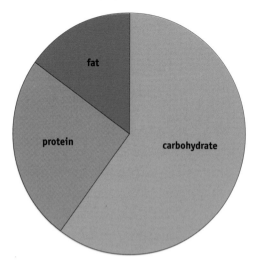

Figure 27: ideal nutritional balance for peak mental and physical fitness

brain foods

Most of the foods mentioned in the basic healthy diet contain various items that are good for the brain (and what is good for your brain is good for your body!) Specifically, the brain and its nervous system are nourished by certain amino acids (the constituents of protein), the B complex of vitamins, the essential fats found abundantly in fish, and the minerals potassium, magnesium, iron and zinc. Any healthy diet should include food that contains these essential nutrients.

The more aerobically fit your body is, the more your digestive system is able to ingest its food, and the more efficiently and effectively your blood can deliver the nutrients to your entire body and brain.

the intelligent diet

The intelligent diet will naturally contain appropriate sugars and salts. It is therefore unnecessary and in many cases harmful to add additional salts and sugars to food (see page 213). Similarly, any refined or processed food will tend to be more difficult to digest, and may contain elements that are damaging to your general health. It is also useful to restrict your intake of dairy and wheat products, neither of which the adult human digestive system is designed to cope with.

●   ●   ●

Now we have seen how diet plays a huge role in our brain and body health, in the next chapter we will see how stress and sleep affect your body, and discuss what effects drugs and your mental attitude can have on your body and brain.

chapter nine

stress-busting, healing, and more...

In order to really grasp the concept that they [patients] can mentally influence their body's immune mechanism, they eventually realised that their mind and emotions and body act as a unit which can't be separated ... that there was a mental and psychological participation, as well as a physical one, in the development of their disease.

Dr. O. Carl Simonton

Having looked at how to keep your external body fit and in shape, and how to keep your body and brain well fed, in this chapter we will see how the fitness of your mind affects the fitness of your body, and the fitness of your body affects the fitness of your mind!

I will show you how stress and sleep affect your body and brain, and some relaxation techniques guaranteed to calm and heal you.

mind and body – stress

Good health, mental and physical, doesn't just rely on good nutrition and good diet, or on exercise. It also relies on our *brains*. How we think and feel emotionally hugely affects how we feel physically, and how fit we are physically impacts considerably on how fit we are mentally.

Your mental attitude has a direct correlation with both your physical health and your mental fitness. An attitude of fear, indecision, indifference, inflexibility, and negativism produces stress, ill health, and a generally deteriorating set of mental skills. Studies by the British Medical Association and the American Medical Association have shown that as much as 80 percent of disease is caused by these negative mental attitudes.

Professor John McLeod of Abertay University, Dundee, studied 10,000 workers in the British private sector for stress levels. His report, given to the British Association for Counselling and Psychotherapy in January 2001, found that stress in the workplace was spiralling out of control. The stress levels were so high that many employees were in danger of completely burning out.

Professor McLeod's survey reported that in most occupations up to 15 percent of staff have problems with stress. Even more seriously, in the vital professions of teaching, social work and the police, one in four employees are suffering from serious stress.

Professor McLeod said: "People who need workplace counselling showed signs of psychological distress equivalent to that found in out–patient psychiatric hospitals."

He confirmed that the increasing problem of work-related stress was no longer confined to management. It now affects office workers and manual workers equally. He further reported that undiagnosed anxiety/stress conditions now caused more absences from work than traditional complaints such as backache, hangovers and stomach trouble.

In our modern age, stress has been one of the major afflictions blighting an increasing number of people's lives. Your physiological response to stress is a biochemical one, and this changed chemistry affects every one of your organs, and therefore by association and reflection, every cell in your body. Both severe stress and continuing strain will therefore be reflected in both physical and mental dis-ease.

In contrast, an open-minded, committed, flexible, curious and optimistic mental attitude will produce a body that is physically more healthy and free from stress, and a mind which is more alert and capable of dealing with the constant "intelligence tests" with which the planet Earth challenges your brain every hour of every day.

The good news is that stress is primarily a mental phenomenon. Why is this good news? Because, as you will now know, if it is a mental phenomenon it can be guided and controlled.

Before launching into methods for controlling unnecessarily high stress levels and producing a more calm and relaxed state for yourself, let's check your current "stress state."

stress-state check

There are three main areas in which you can check your current stress levels: physical, behavioral, and psychological.

Go through the following questionnaire, and then check your results below. Answer "YES" if the statement generally applies to you; "NO" if the statement generally does not apply to you.

	YES	NO

Physical

I regularly have heart palpitations

I am often breathless

I suffer from general aches and pains with no
   apparent cause

I have consistent backaches

I often get colds or other minor infections

I often feel as if things are going out of focus
   and that I might faint

I have constant skin complaints

My hands are usually clammy

I sweat a lot

I often feel tightness or pains in my chest

For no apparent reasons my muscles will suddenly
   begin to twitch

I fidget a lot

I suffer from regular indigestion

I often have constipation or diarrhea

I suffer from constant headaches/migraines

I generally feel tired and fatigued

I often feel weak at the knees

In the morning my body often feels too heavy to
   get out of bed

Behavioral

I regularly grind my teeth

I constantly clench my fists

I either eat a lot for "comfort" or lose my appetite
   for no apparent reason

	YES	NO
My sleep is irregular and disturbed		
I rush things, especially eating and talking		
I feel too busy to take time for relaxation		
I am smoking more than usual		
My intake of caffeine/alcohol is increasing		
I am becoming more irritable, especially with other people and minor events		
My time management is weak to non-existent		
My efficiency at work or in projects is not at its peak		
I am tending to become more withdrawn and less outgoing		
I am becoming more aggressive		
My behavior is becoming more compulsive		
My movements are becoming more quick and jerky		
My attention seldom rests for more than a few seconds on any one thing		
Psychological		
I would describe myself as generally melancholic or depressed		
With others I often feel embarrassed, ashamed and "less than them"		
I feel generally weak and helpless		
I feel that I am controlled by others more than I should		
I have regular mood swings, often sudden and violent		
I have nightmares that wake me from sleep		

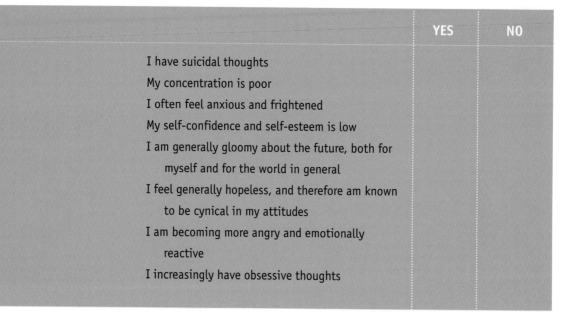

	YES	NO
I have suicidal thoughts		
My concentration is poor		
I often feel anxious and frightened		
My self-confidence and self-esteem is low		
I am generally gloomy about the future, both for myself and for the world in general		
I feel generally hopeless, and therefore am known to be cynical in my attitudes		
I am becoming more angry and emotionally reactive		
I increasingly have obsessive thoughts		

analysis

If you answered "yes" more times than you did "no" in any of the three sections, your stress levels are above average. If you have more than 10 "yes" answers, your stress levels are particularly high.

It would be useful for you to check your answers to find out what is the underlying cause of each of your positive responses. To help you with this analysis, read through the following chart. It was designed by Dr. Selye, a Swiss expert on stress and the body's reactions to it. Dr. Selye realized that certain standard events in life will cause the body to release "stress chemicals." He then worked out a stress rating scale, which will enable you rapidly to check your own "stress score" and, with the help of Head Strong, to adjust your behavior appropriately.

stress social readjustment rating scale

Event	Value
Death of spouse	100
Divorce	73
Marital separation	65
Jail term	63
Death of close family member	63
Personal injury or illness	53
Marriage	50
Fired from work	47
Marital reconciliation	45
Retirement	45
Change in family member's health	44
Pregnancy	40
Sexual difficulties	39
Addition to family	39
Business readjustment	39
Change in financial status	38
Death of a close friend	37
Change to different line of work	36
Change in number of marital arguments	35
Large mortgage or loan	31
Foreclosure of mortgage or loan	30
Change in work responsibilities	29
Son or daughter leaving home	29
Trouble with in-laws	29
Outstanding personal achievement	28
Spouse begins or stops work	26
Starting or finishing school	26

Change in living conditions	25
Revision of personal habits	24
Trouble with the boss	23
Change in work hours, conditions	20
Change in residence	20
Change in schools	20
Change in recreational habits	19
Change in church activities	19
Change in social activities	18
Small mortgage or loan	17
Change in sleeping habits	16
Change in number of family gatherings	15
Change in eating habits	15
Holiday	13
Minor violation of the law	11

Now that you know your own stress levels and their probable causes, let's look first at the relationship between stress and aerobic fitness, and then at some other **Good New Habits** you can establish in order to make your life more relaxed, calm, peaceful and productive.

A study by Dean Ornish, Head of the Preventative Medicine Research Institute in Saratoga, California, has confirmed that high stress levels caused by cynical attitudes and emotions can cause negative biological responses that lead to coronary heart disease. In the 1980s, Dr. Redford Williams, a behavior medicine specialist at Duke University Medical Center, and his colleagues examined the health records of 255 medical students that had been collected 25 years earlier. Those students who had showed high animosity on a scale called a "Hostility Inventory" were found to have been seven times more likely to develop heart disease or die by the age of 50.

"I think the mind is where the heart disease begins for many people," states Dr. Ornish, who on the basis of these findings is developing programs to reduce stress and, therefore, reverse heart disease. His method? Exercises including meditation and yoga in order to reshape emotions and behavior; healthy diets; and reducing all drug taking, especially smoking.

Using this approach Dr. Ornish reported that the majority of his patients with serious heart ailments were able actually to unplug their clogged arteries.

aerobic fitness and stress

Aerobic fitness significantly affects stress levels, reducing them dramatically. When you are aerobically unfit, you have a smaller, weaker heart that pumps "flop, flop, flop, flop, flop, flop, flop, flop, flop, flop ..." at an agitated and nervous-making 80 or more beats per minute. With each weak beat it is increasing the probability that your blood carrying arteries, veins and capillaries will continue to constrict, is providing your lungs and digestive system with little energy or help to perform their vital tasks, and is providing all other parts of your body, especially your muscles and brain, with a low quality, low-octane fuel.

Your aerobically fit heart has a totally different rhythm and effect: "BOOOHHM!...BOOOHHM!...BOOOHHM!...BOOOHHM!...BOOOHHM!" With each gigantic beat a high octane 5-star fuel nourishes and cleanses the lungs and digestive system, revitalizes the neuro-muscular system and feeds the brain with invigorating energy.

Also, with each beat the cardiovascular system gently swells and subsides. When you are aerobically fit your heart and blood give you a soothing and comforting internal massage 60 times a minute! Aerobic fitness is one of the quickest and most natural ways of reducing stress and bringing about a feeling of relaxation, calm and physical and psychological well-being.

In which of these two bodies would your brain prefer to exist?!

stress busting!

Why is it that of all the animals, human beings seem to suffer from more stress than the others?

Why *don't* animals, especially the hunted such as deer, suffer from stress?

The answer is that they *do*. It's just that the stress they experience is positive and short in duration. When the deer is under threat, its body is exquisitely designed to erupt in a cascade of chemicals that pour energy and alertness into and throughout its body system. Massive amounts of energy are suddenly available and are mobilized for immediate action. This results in the commonly known "fight or flight" response, and it is one that we are programmed for as well.

During this high stress, high tension, high action time, all stable, long-term growth and repair activities of the body are held in suspension. As soon as the hunt is over, the surviving animals immediately reduce their hormone levels, and revert to the more stable long-term survival physiological balance.

The problem for we humans is that in modern society we tend to worry *constantly* – about social relationships, examinations, finances, social standing, job advancement, pollution, crime, the general state of the world…

This places a constant stress on the system, and we are consequently in the "alert" mode, causing a physiological chaos that eventually results in system break-down.

Continuing stress, or even heavy short-term stress, will affect the immune system which ensures that the body's foot soldiers are ready to annihilate any marauding organisms or incipient cancers. A person with a damaged immune system will be prey to infections and malignancies. Sir William Ogilvie, a famous surgeon during my youth, claimed that by looking around a board room or committee table and assessing the degree of stress which was affecting his colleagues, he could guess who would be a future patient.

Dr. Thomas Stuttaford, Medical Advisor, *The Times*

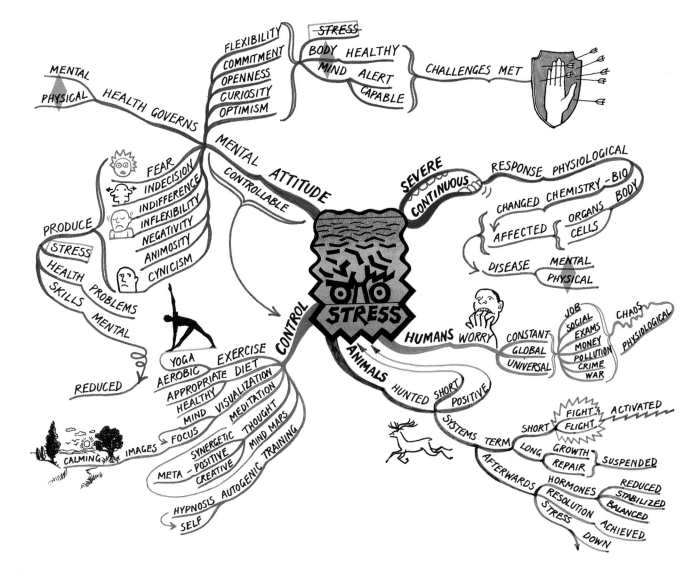

Mind Map® 17

The good news is that once you are aware how stress affects your body and brain, you can control it!

Head Strong has introduced you to some techniques that will have already been adjusting your stress levels positively: **Synergetic Thinking**; **Meta-Positive Thinking**; Mind Mapping®; **Creative Thinking**; and Physical Exercise and appropriate Nutrition.

There are three additional techniques you can use which are specifically devoted to reducing your stress levels: Visualization; Autogenic Training; and Meditation.

What follows is a Stress Management Workout that will have far ranging and beneficial psychological, physical and behavioral effects.

In our privileged lives, we are uniquely smarter enough to have invented psychological stressors, and uniquely foolish enough to let them dominate our lives.

I am in broad agreement ... that we, as individuals, have the potential to manage our stress response, especially that created by florid imaginations cogitating future events.

Barry Keverne, Director of the Department of Animal Behavior, University of Cambridge

stress reduction techniques

visualization

Visualization is a technique for focusing your mind on calming or beneficial images, which remove you from the stressful "chatter" that often dominates the mind.

To practice visualization techniques effectively, make sure that you are comfortable, with your body ideally in a state of comparative ease. When you are in this state, try the following visualization, taking yourself progressively through the five stages. For the first few practices, spend only five minutes or so on it, and concentrate on the first two stages. As you progress, advance to the third, fourth and fifth levels, spending as much time as you wish.

stage 1

Close your eyes and rotate your eyeballs upward and inward, as if you were "internally looking" at the center of your forehead. This position, for reasons that are still being explored, produces a relaxed and "drifting" feeling, while preparing your brain for internal visualization.

stage 2

With your eyes in this upward position, choose a specific color and try to fill your internal visual field and universe with it. Depending on your moods and preferences, you may choose colors such as blue and green, which will give you a cool feeling, or colors such as red, orange, yellow and purple, which are more warm.

Once you have mastered this, you can begin to experiment with visualizing different geometric shapes such as circles, squares, and triangles, coloring them differently at your own whim.

Next you can make it into a wonderful playground by adding movement to the shapes – tumbling, turning, lifting, raising and increasing the size of your kaleidoscopic internal universe.

All the time you are doing this, your mind and body will be becoming increasingly relaxed and at ease.

stage 3

The next stage is your "favorite" object/s visualization. In this you choose an object that comes "naturally" to your internal mind and which you find particularly pleasing. The focus in this part of the visualization is to hold that object as clearly as you can in your mind, for as long as you can. It doesn't matter if it floats in and out of your consciousness – which it will. The object of the exercise is to keep it present for as often and as long as you can.

stage 4

In this stage you graduate from a specific object to the visualization of abstract subjects and their transformation into different and subtle images.

For example, you might decide on concepts such as beauty, freedom, happiness or justice. You can start this stage by simply visualizing the word, and progress to hearing it either spoken or from the "ether." As the visualization progresses, imagine beautiful and elegant symbols that can form icons for the abstract idea. Then progress to make wonderful stories and allegories about the subject you are visualizing.

A particularly useful visualization at this stage is to create your own internal Mind-Map (in three dimensions!) around the topic.

stage 5 – universal harmony

The fifth stage of the visualization is to create visual manifestations for giant overall feelings of peace and wellbeing. Imagine the feeling you would have while standing on the top of Mount Everest looking over the Himalayas. Then create the visualization. Bring nature to the fore at this advanced stage, and use her stage props of sunsets, other planets, and giant natural vistas to give you this expansive feeling and visualization. Imagining yourself flying in such situations can also be useful for this stage.

Cancer patients who undergo relaxation and hypnotherapy as well as conventional chemotherapy can live up to two-and-a-half times longer than those receiving chemotherapy on its own. These are the findings of a study headed by Leslie Walker of Hull University, England, on 63 patients who all had cancer of the lymph system, known as Hodgkin's disease. The study of the survival rates of the 63 patients in Scotland found that 13 years after diagnosis and treatment, those who had received training in simple relaxation techniques, some so basic as simply closing the eyes and recalling a time when they were happy and secure, have significantly higher survival rates.

autogenic training

Autogenic training, or auto-hypnosis, is a technique for self-relaxation and self-**Meta-Positive** programming that allows the incredible power of your cerebral cortex to communicate directly with your "lower brain" (see pages 16 to 22).

Make sure that you are lying on your back in a warm and comfortable place (ideally on a couch or bed), or that you are sitting very comfortably in a supporting chair that allows you to relax all your limbs and muscles.

Once you are in this position, take 10 long and deep breaths, feeling your increasing relaxation, especially as you exhale.

After you have completed the 10 breaths, close your eyes and once again roll them up so that you are "looking at the inside of your forehead."

In this state, you take a very gentle tour from the tip of your toes to the top of your head. On the tour you focus your internal vision on each part of your body successively. As you "arrive" at each one, you give it gentle instructions to become calm, relaxed, peaceful, warm and still, while "feeling" it obeying. As you do this, feel that particular part of your body sinking more comfortably into your bed, couch or chair.

When you have finished with your feet, move up to your ankles, lower legs, knees, thighs, groin, hips, lower back, middle back, upper back, stomach, ribcage, throat, neck, shoulders, upper arms, elbows, forearms, palms, fingers, scull, eyes (make sure you feel the lids heavy), jaw, mouth, and tongue.

When your entire body is relaxed, you then communicate, through your lower brain, with your upper brain, using one of your most important or favorite Brain Boosters. While you are in this state the communication between the two parts of your brain will be much more efficient, since all the "static" of your normal active thoughts and sensory processing has been removed.

The advantage of this exercise is that it takes only a few minutes, and is a wonderful refresher during the day. An ideal "dose" would be three to four times daily.

If you are not certain which Brain Booster to choose, the best general one is:

Every day in every way I am getting better and better

because this instructs your massively powerful autonomic (naturally functioning) nervous system to increase its activity in making you more physically and mentally healthy.

During the training period, keep repeating the Brain Booster to yourself, between 20 and 100 times.

As you now know, while you are doing this, you will be establishing magnificently a **Good New Habit/Meta-Positive Thinking Habit.** Autogenic/self-hypnotic training is the best way for you to do this.

meditation

Meditation is simply an experiential exercise which involves the focusing of your attention; it is not a belief system, although most spiritual schools of thought highly recommend and practice this thinking art.

During meditation, the brain becomes "detached" from standard reality, and enters a state of calm and peaceful awareness in which alpha waves (the brain's open/receptive/calm waves) predominate.

Our realization of this came about as a result of the seminal study by two Japanese psychiatrists, Kasamatsu and Hirai, who in 1966 did an extensive study on four Zen masters. The study showed that:

- Alpha waves predominated in the EEG records of the Zen masters.
- Drowsiness was ruled out as being responsible for the state of deep relaxation achieved, because the EEG records were also monitored for sleep onset and showed no indication of it.
- The alpha waves persisted even when the Zen masters had their eyes open (this is a condition virtually impossible for the average person to maintain with open eyes).

The conclusion of the study was that a focused attention on dreaming would greatly enhance general well-being and creative output. This is confirmed in the lives of those with great minds, where dreaming and fantasy are often the wellsprings for great new ideas and paradigm shifts in concepts.

In a well-exercised and well-fed body, sleep will be deep and curative, and will often provide, from an infinite source of creativity, major insights and revelations.

drugs and addiction

The word "drugs" conjures up a host of fears and evils, and it is true that the addictive drugs heroin, cocaine, crack, ecstasy and marijuana, generally have major negative effects on the human nervous system. Their possible side-effects include memory loss, paranoia, neurological damage, social maladaptability, depression and death. Occasionally they can be prescribed under expert supervision. However, the two drugs named as the most dangerous by the United Nations are nicotine and alcohol; both of which are used socially almost mandatorily, and both of which have significant effects on the brain and the body.

nicotine

Every time nicotine is inhaled, a yellowish-brown coating of oil smothers the 600,000,000 alveoli of the lungs, making it far more difficult for oxygen to pass through into the bloodstream, and therefore depriving the brain of some of its vital energy supply. Cigarette smoking tends to lead to a general increase in upper respiratory and cardiovascular ailments, with a markedly greater probability of suffering major illnesses such as cancer and coronary heart disease, with a corresponding reduction in life-expectancy.

alcohol

A useful way to look at this drug is to take the perspective of a Martian, examining the effects of varying amounts of this particular liquid on the brain, nervous system and muscular system of the inhabitants of Earth. Prolonged use causes massive memory loss, disintegration of vital organs, vocabulary and language impairment, disintegration of the muscular system, eventual loss of brain cells, loss of balance and coordination, and a life expectancy reduced by as much as 30 years.

On the up-side for those readers who enjoy the odd drink, studies have shown that moderate drinking, especially when the drink is taken with food, combined with good exercise, can relax the mind and body, and may even in some instances be helpful to the cardiovascular system. Some studies show that those who drink in moderation (a couple of glasses of wine, with food, per day) have an additional two years' life expectancy.

As with the advice on diet, it is essential to "listen" to your body's real needs. For parents-to-be it is especially important to realize that alcohol is the main drug to which a fetus can become addicted during pregnancy. This is partly because alcohol is the only major drug that is both water and fat soluble, and therefore, insidiously, invades the child's entire body and brain system.

Your body and brain are unbelievably complex and delicately balanced eco-systems, all working to maintain the equilibrium that gives balance, stability and energy to your life. Drugs of all sorts – medical or recreational – will usually have complex mind and body changing influences on you. Treat them and your body and brain with care.

abuse – a problem of thinking

In dealing with the global drug addiction problem, the human race has developed and is continuing to develop a growing and incredibly dangerous **Meta-Negative Thinking Habit**. This habit revolves around the concept "abuse."

Anyone taking an illegal, addictive drug is labelled a drug abuser. The taking of drugs is labelled drug abuse. A global army of medics, social workers, politicians and teachers rails against this global curse.

Their morals are right.

Their thinking is dangerously wrong.

The very term "drug abuse" allows the drug abuser the safety of non-involvement in the description of his or her activity – it is the drugs that are being abused, not the user, and who cares if you line up some samples of heroin, crack or cocaine and spit and swear at them! If the phrase were changed to "self abuse with drugs," the thinking patterns and emotional reactions of both users and society would change, and the situation would be seen in a more realistic light. It would be even more so if everyone were aware of just how miraculous the body and brain are that are the object and subject of the abuse.

Another major thinking danger relating to drugs concerns the globally popular phrases which take the form of "once a ..., always a ... !" You can fill them in with numerous words such as "smoker," "addict," "alcoholic," etc.

These **Meta-Negative Thinking Habits** are both invidious and incorrect – they are not the truth. The truth is that an alcoholic who stops drinking is a non-alcoholic who has a higher probability, both physical and psychological, of drinking alcohol.

If everyone knew this, the reformed smoker or alcoholic who momentarily relapsed would not collapse in an agony of self-abuse, defeat and hopelessness, as is often the case. They would realize that they had had a momentary *Event* that took them away from their intended goal. This thinking makes it much more easy to return to a healthy path (see Chapter 6, page 117).

Health and relaxation expert Leslie Kenton reports research in the United States involving 2,000 students between the ages of 19 and 23. The students were taught to practice regular meditation, and continued their practice for periods ranging from a few months to two years.

The remarkable findings were as follows: the reduction of negative habit patterns such as drug taking (of both prescription and mind-altering drugs), alcohol consumption and cigarette smoking was dramatic. One particularly noticeable statistic was that the number of smokers reduced by half during the first six months of meditation. Approximately one year later the number was down to one third.

The significant point about these findings was that the reductions in self-destructive behavior were completely spontaneous. Throughout the entire duration of the study the experimenters had made no suggestion, nor had given any instruction referring to the fact that relaxation or meditation would or should affect in any way these negative and addictive habits.

brain foods

From what you have read so far in this and the preceding chapters, you will be able to deduce that your brain, in order to survive and be well, requires four major "Brain Foods."

1. **Oxygen** – This is your brain's prime energy source, and is only provided in the quantities required by a physically fit and healthy body.
2. **Nutrition** – Your brain needs a regular supply of the appropriate vitamins, minerals and other nutrients. These are essential to keep the giant bio-chemical laboratory that is your brain functioning at full efficiency. Make sure your diet is excellent.
3. **Information** – Your brain needs a constant flow of "info-food," which it must receive through its senses and its intellectual skills. Make sure that

you keep your senses alert, and that you enthusiastically embrace lifelong learning.

4. **Love** – Without it your brain will wither. Ensure you have a plentiful supply!

You are about to become a graduate of *Head Strong*! As such you will be among the privileged members of the human race to have an integrated knowledge and understanding of the relationship between the human brain and the human body – the branch of knowledge known as **Holanthropy**.

"This knowledge" and its application include (and here comes your Meta-Summary of *Head Strong*!):

- The fact that the human brain is **Synergetic** and has an infinite potential for the generation of thought, **Creative Thinking**, and the solution of all problems.
- The ability of the upper brain to control all the other parts of the brain.
- The multiple "fingers of intelligence" of the left and right cortex, which, when used in harmony, multiply a hundred-fold your overall brain power and effectiveness.

- The knowledge that the brain is still comprehensively and commandingly more powerful and intelligent than any array of the world's most powerful super-computers, and that they can be used to enhance and multiply the human multiple intelligences.
- The ingrained, cellular awareness of the number of brain cells, each brain cell's astonishing capability, and the limitless power they have when acting for you in concert and harmony.
- The full mastery of **Meta-Positive Thinking** and the **Meta-Positive Thinking Formula**, including understanding how to make use of the **Big Bad Habits** and the **Meta-Negative Thinking Habits** to build wisdom and experience of life.
- A deep knowledge of the processes of **Creative Thinking** and the practiced ability to make lightning-fast and multiple associations between anything and anything else.
- A full understanding of the multi-ordinate nature of words, the extraordinary uniqueness of every human being and their infinite capacity for **Association**, and the application of this aspect of mental literacy to the understanding of self and others.
- A comprehensive grasp of the ultimate thinking tool – the **Mind Map**®, and the application of this "Swiss army-knife of the brain" to analytical, strategic, lateral, radiant, and global thinking in all its forms.
- The complete integration of the **Ultimate Learning Success Formula – TEFCAS** – into all aspects of life.
- Acceptance and application of the **Brain Principle of Success**, as applied to the individual and to all group communications, activities and projects.
- The persistent application of **Brain Principle of Persistence**!
- A full understanding of the structure and nature of the human body, including the knowledge of the astonishing statistics about the make-up of its constituent parts.
- A mastery of the concepts of general physical fitness, and the practice and development of **Poise, Flexibility, Aerobic fitness**, and **Strength**.

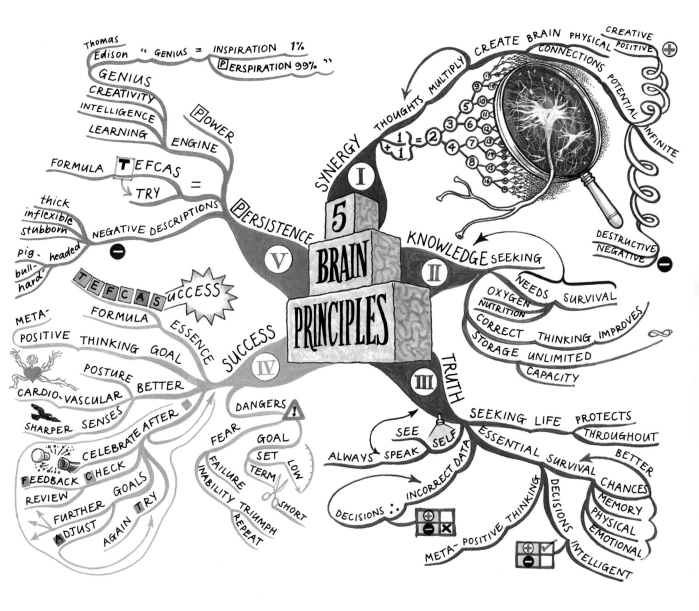

Thomas Edison " GENIUS = INSPIRATION 1% PERSPIRATION 99% "

SYNERGY THOUGHTS MULTIPLY CREATE BRAIN PHYSICAL CONNECTIONS POTENTIAL

CREATIVE POSITIVE ⊕

INFINITE

DESTRUCTIVE NEGATIVE ⊖

$+\frac{1}{1} = 2$

I

GENIUS
CREATIVITY
INTELLIGENCE
LEARNING

POWER ENGINE

FORMULA **T** EFCAS =

→ TRY

5 BRAIN PRINCIPLES

thick
inflexible
stubborn
pig- headed
bull-
hard-

NEGATIVE DESCRIPTIONS ⊖

PERSISTENCE

V

KNOWLEDGE SEEKING

II

NEEDS SURVIVAL
OXYGEN
NUTRITION
CORRECT THINKING IMPROVES
STORAGE UNLIMITED
CAPACITY

∞

T E F C A S UCCESS

META-
POSITIVE THINKING GOAL

FORMULA ESSENCE

SUCCESS

IV

POSTURE BETTER
CARDIO- VASCULAR

SHARPER SENSES

CELEBRATE AFTER

FEEDBACK CHECK
REVIEW
FURTHER GOALS
ADJUST AGAIN TRY

DANGERS ⚠

TRUTH

III

SEEKING LIFE PROTECTS
THROUGHOUT
ESSENTIAL SURVIVAL BETTER
CHANCES
MEMORY
PHYSICAL
EMOTIONAL
INTELLIGENT

SEE SELF
ALWAYS SPEAK
INCORRECT DATA
DECISIONS ∴

FEAR GOAL
FAILURE SET
INABILITY TRIUMPH TERM LOW
REPEAT SHORT

DECISIONS

META- POSITIVE THINKING

⊕ ☐
⊖ ✗

⊕ ✓
⊖

Mind Map® 18

- A similar mastery of all information pertaining to the best and most appropriate science for maintaining the body/mind system.

Armed with this knowledge you will find life becomes more interesting, more positively challenging, more exciting and more rewarding.

Like a series of internal compasses, the principles and formulas you have learned through your reading of *Head Strong* will give you additional balance, focus and direction throughout your life.

You belong to an *incredible* Body Thinking race! You are one of its *incredible* Body Thinking members.

Floreant Dendritae!

(Let your Brain Cells Flourish!)